MW01488390

INSTRUCTOR'S RESOURCE MANUAL

Suzanne E. Hughes
Florida Community College at Jacksonville

Patti Levine-Brown
Florida Community College at Jacksonville

EMPOWERED COLLEGE
READING
MOTIVATION MATTERS

FIRST EDITION

Linda A. Lee
San Diego Miramar College

PEARSON
Prentice
Hall

Upper Saddle River, New Jersey 07458

This work is protected by United States copyright laws and is provided *solely for the use of instructors* in teaching their courses and assessing student learning. Dissemination or sale of any part of this work *(including on the World Wide Web)* will destroy the integrity of the work and is not permitted. The work and materials from it should never be made available to students except by instructors using the accompanying text in their classes. All recipients of this work are expected to abide by these restrictions and to honor the intended pedagogical purposes and the needs of other instructors who rely on these materials.

© 2008 by PEARSON EDUCATION, INC.
Upper Saddle River, New Jersey 07458

All rights reserved

10 9 8 7 6 5 4 3 2 1

ISBN 10: 0-13-183896-2
ISBN 13: 978-0-13-183896-3

Printed in the United States of America

Table of Contents

Dear Instructor,

Thank you for choosing *Empowered College Reading, Motivation Matters*! This **Instructor's Resource Manual** is packed with tools to help you make the most of this text with your students. In addition to the resources printed within the pages of this manual, we have also provided several resources electronically via the included **Instructor's Resource CD** and the **Instructor Resource Center** located at www.prenhall.com. The **Instructor's Resource CD** contains ALL of the printed resources included in this manual, as well as chapter-specific **PowerPoint Presentations** intended for classroom use, and *The Prentice Hall Reading Skills Test Bank*, an additional resource for generating tests and quizzes. In addition, the **Textbook Answer Key** is available for instructor download from www.prenhall.com. Instructions for registering and downloading the **Textbook Answer Key,** as well as all other Prentice Hall supplements appear on pages vii-xii of this manual.

We sincerely hope you will find these resources helpful while planning and teaching your course.

Thanks for choosing Prentice Hall!

Instructor Resource Center
Getting Registered

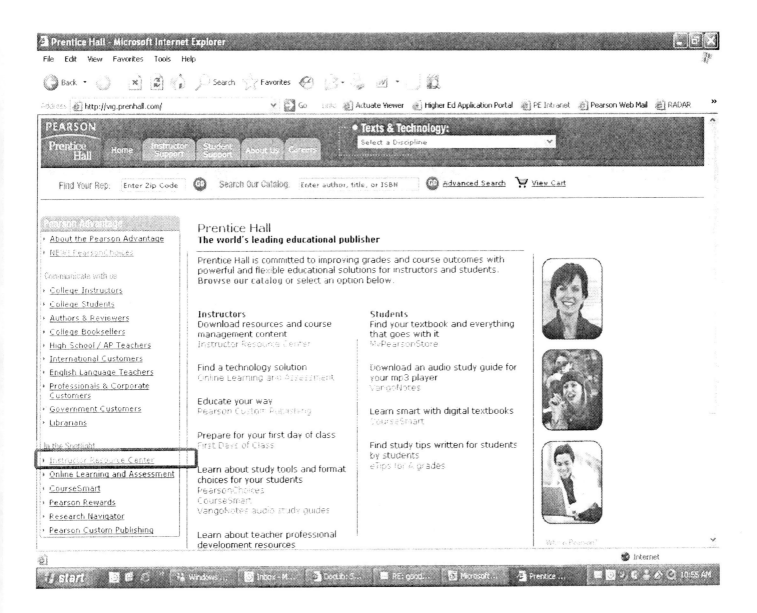

To register for the Pearson Instructor Resource Center, go to the homepage for your textbook's publisher.

1. Click "**Instructor Resource Center**" on the left navigation.

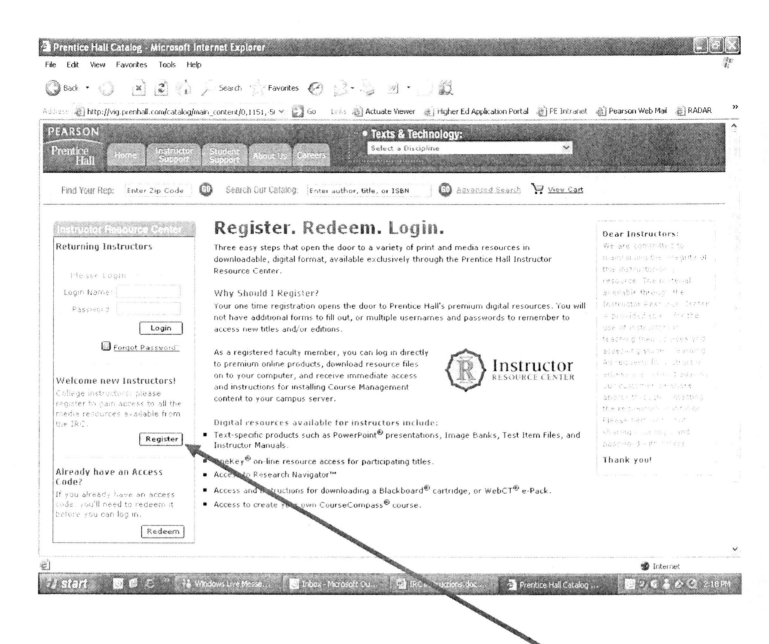

2. To request access to download digital supplements, click the "**Register**" button.

Follow the provided instructions. Once you have been verified as a valid Pearson instructor, an instructor code will be emailed to you. Please use this code to set up your Pearson login name and password.

Instructor Resource Center
Downloading Resources

PEARSON
Prentice Hall | Home | Instructor Support | Student Support | About Us | Careers

• Texts & Technology: Select a Discipline

Find Your Rep: Enter Zip Code GO   Search Our Catalog: Enter author, title, or ISBN GO   Advanced Search   View Cart

1. Go to www.prenhall.com and click the **Advanced Search** option located at the top of the page.

Advanced Catalog Search

KEYWORD:

TITLE: Empowered College Reading

AUTHOR:

ISBN:

EDITION:

SERIES:

2. Use the **Advanced Catalog Search** to find the catalog page for your text.

3. Select your text from the provided results.

New Search

Title

Empowered College Reading: Motivation Matters, 1/e
Lee
©2008 | Prentice Hall | Paper; 592 pp | Instock
ISBN-10: 0131838938 | ISBN-13: 9780131838932

ABOUT THIS PRODUCT
- Description
- Table of Contents
- Features
- New To This Edition
- Sample Chapter
- Alternate Version(s)

PACKAGE OPTIONS
- Valuepack(s)

RESOURCES
- Student
- Instructor
- Course-Specific
- Discipline-Specific

INTERNET RESOURCES
- Companion Website

4. After being directed to the catalog page for your text, click the **Instructor** link located under **Resources** on the left-side navigation bar.

By clicking the Instructor link, all of the book-specific print and digital resources for your text will be listed below the main title.

Items available for download will have a ⊞ icon.

5. Click the highlighted file name of the version you want to download.

Instructor's Resource Manual
Hughes & Levine-Brown
© 2008 | Prentice Hall | Paper; 320 pages | Estimated Availability: 10/01/2007
ISBN-10: 0131838962 | ISBN-13: 9780131838963
The Instructor's Resource Manual for *Empowered College Reading* will help instru
text. Resources include chapter summaries, two 15-question multiple-choice quiz
chapter. In addition, there are three 50-question diagnostic tests of reading skills
complete textbook chapters on the CD-ROM.

⊞ Instructor's Resource Manual (1.5MB | zip file | Type: Manuals/Guides) ❷
Instructor's Resource Manual to accompany Empowered College Reading: Moti

You will be prompted to login with an Instructor Resource Center login.

6. Enter your login name & password, and click the **"Log In"** button.

Instructor Resource Center Log In

Welcome Educators!

To download instructor resources or request course content from this site, you must log in using your personal Pearson Education account (Login Name and Password).

Returning Instructors, Welcome Back

If you already have a valid Login Name and Password, please enter it here. If you have previously registered for access to a Pearson product (such as Supplements Central, MathXL or CourseCompass), try the same login name and password here.

If you have already received an access code but have not yet redeemed it; please click here to register and create your Login Name and Password.

Login Name: [   ]
Password: [   ]   [Forgot your login/password?]
[Log In] [Cancel]

7. Read the terms and conditions and then click the **"I accept"** button to begin the download process.

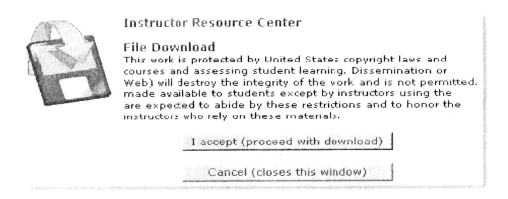

Instructor Resource Center

File Download
This work is protected by United States copyright laws and courses and assessing student learning. Dissemination or Web) will destroy the integrity of the work and is not permitted. made available to students except by instructors using the are expected to abide by these restrictions and to honor the instructors who rely on these materials.

I accept (proceed with download)

Cancel (closes this window)

8. **"Save"** the supplement file to a folder you can easily find again.

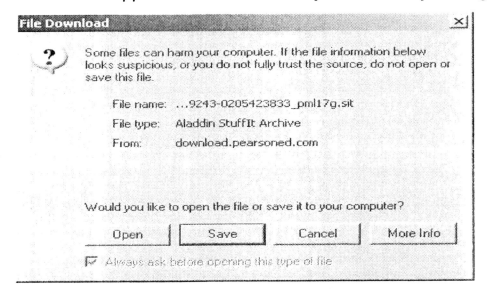

File Download

Some files can harm your computer. If the file information below looks suspicious, or you do not fully trust the source, do not open or save this file.

File name: ...9243-0205423833_pml17g.sit

File type: Aladdin StuffIt Archive

From: download.pearsoned.com

Would you like to open the file or save it to your computer?

Open | Save | Cancel | More Info

Always ask before opening this type of file

Once you are signed into the IRC, you may then continue to download additional resources from our online catalog.

For security purposes, please "Sign Out" when you are finished!

A Few Notes...

1. Be sure to turn off your **Pop-Up Blocker** prior to downloading supplements. If your blocker is left on you will not be able to download files from www.prenhall.com.

2. All files posted to the Instructor Resource Center are in a **compressed** format. After you have saved the compressed folder to your hard drive, you will need to use **WinZip** or **StuffIt** software to expand and view the files.

SAMPLE 10-WEEK SYLLABUS

Term/Year:	
Reference Number:	
Instructor:	
Office:	
E-mail:	
Phone Number:	
Web Page:	
Classroom:	

REQUIRED TEXTBOOK:
Empowered College Reading by Linda Lee

COURSE DESCRIPTION: This reading course is designed to enhance basic reading skills, develop higher-level vocabulary and comprehension skills, textbook reading techniques, and learning strategies needed for success in college. Students must satisfy appropriate exit level scores in addition to the coursework in order to complete this course successfully.

COURSE PREREQUISITIES: Satisfactory score on standardized test or satisfactory completion of other required reading courses.

LEARNING OUTCOMES: In this advanced level reading course students prepare for college-level reading by learning strategies and study skills to help them become more efficient and effective readers. Throughout the course, students will achieve the following learning outcomes

- Demonstrate an improved vocabulary
- Recognize the main idea
- Identify the topic sentence
- Identify supporting details
- Identify the implied main idea
- Recognize patterns of organization
- Detect bias
- Identify logical inferences
- Distinguish between fact and opinion
- Recognize the author's purpose
- Demonstrate improved reading efficiency
- Pass the State Exit Exam

STATE EXIT EXAM: Students in Florida must take the Florida State Exit Exam before exiting this class. In order to pass the exam, students must answer 23 of the 36 questions on the exam correctly. This minimum score must be achieved prior to receiving a grade in this class, regardless of how high you may have scored on class assignments or tests. In other words, you cannot pass this course unless you pass the State Exit Exam.

CLASSROOM ARRANGEMENT AND METHOD OF INSTRUCTION: In this class students will be divided into Cooperative Learning groups. Each group member is asked to participate to the fullest extent on group assignments and projects. Students will receive both

group and individual grades. Additionally, students will receive instruction through lectures, class discussions, peer instruction, audio/video materials, written assignments, and oral reports.

GRADES: Methods used to document a students' mastery of course performance will be teacher observations, classroom assignments, group assignments, and examinations. Reading is a skills-based course and a large percentage of class time will be spent practicing the skills introduced and discussed in class. Since much of the course work will be done in class, students need to make an effort to attend every class. Grades for the course will be determined in the following manner:

1. Class Assignments - 25%
2. Vocabulary Tests - 25%
3. Group Assignments -25%
4. Lab Activities - 25%

GRADING SCALE:
90 – 100   A
80 – 89   B
70 – 79   C
Averages below 70 will be recorded as an F

READING LABS: Students will complete a series of lab activities for this class.

IMPORTANT COLLEGE DATES

CALENDAR OF ACTIVITIES

Week	Topic	Activities/Assignments
Week 1	Course Introduction Chapter 1 The Power of Motivation	• Interest Inventory • Learning Styles Inventory • Read the chapter on The Power of Motivation • Complete assignments outlined by the instructor • Participate in discussion activities • Complete vocabulary assignments outlined by the instructor • Chapter test • Journal assignment • Group Activity

Week 2	Chapter 2 **Active Reading** Chapter 3 **Reading Efficiently**	• Read the chapter on Active Reading • Read the chapter on Reading Efficiently • Complete assignments outlined by the instructor • Participate in discussion activities • Complete vocabulary assignments outlined by the instructor • Begin lab assignments outlined by the instructor • Chapter test • Journal assignment • Group Activity
Week 3	Chapter 4 **Vocabulary Expansion** Chapter 5 **Reading for Learning Methods**	• Read the chapter on Vocabulary Expansion • Read the chapter on Reading for Learning Complete assignments outlined by the instructor • Participate in discussion activities • Complete vocabulary assignments outlined by the instructor. • Complete lab assignments outlined by the instructor • Chapter test • Journal assignment • Group Activity
Week 4	Chapter 6 **Main Ideas**	• Read the chapter on Main Ideas • Complete assignments outlined by the instructor • Participate in discussion activities • Complete vocabulary assignments outlined by the instructor • Complete lab assignments outlined by the instructor • Journal assignment • Group Activity
Week 5	Chapter 7 **Details and Logical Patterns**	• Read the chapter on Details and Logical Patterns • Complete assignments outlined by the instructor • Participate in discussion activities • Complete vocabulary assignments outlined by the instructor • Complete lab assignments outlined by the instructor • Journal assignment • Group Activity
Week 6	Chapter 8 **Graphic Aids**	• Read the chapter on Graphic Aids • Complete assignments outlined by the instructor • Participate in discussion activities • Complete vocabulary assignments outlined by the instructor • Chapter test • Journal assignment • Group Activity

Week 7	Chapter 9 Drawing Conclusions	• Read the chapter on Drawing Conclusions • Complete assignments outlined by the instructor • Participate in discussion activities • Complete vocabulary assignments outlined by the instructor • Chapter test • Journal assignment • Group Activity
Week 8	Chapter 10 Evaluating Argument	• Read the chapter on Evaluating Argument • Complete assignments outlined by the instructor • Participate in discussion activities • Complete vocabulary assignments outlined by the instructor • Complete lab assignments outlined by the instructor • Chapter test • Journal assignment • Group Activity
Week 9	Review Reading and Study Strategies and Test Taking Skills Administer Final Exam	• Review Study Strategies and Test Taking Skills with students • Review materials for final exam • Practice test for the State Exit Exam • Administer State Exit Exam. If you must take a state exit please note that the test contains questions related to the skill areas you have reviewed in this course. The test is timed. • Lab assignments to be completed
Week 10	Final Exam State Exit Exam Student-Teacher Conferences	• Administer final exam • If you did not pass the State Exit Exam, you will be given another chance to take a different form of the same test. Please talk with your instructor to schedule a time to come in and take the exam. • Participate in a student-teacher conference about the course

Term/Year:	
Reference Number:	
Instructor:	
Office:	
E-mail:	
Phone Number:	
Web Page:	
Classroom:	

REQUIRED TEXTBOOK:
Empowered College Reading by Linda Lee

COURSE DESCRIPTION: This reading course is designed to enhance basic reading skills, develop higher-level vocabulary and comprehension skills, textbook reading techniques, and learning strategies needed for success in college. Students must satisfy appropriate exit level scores in addition to the coursework in order to complete this course successfully.

COURSE PREREQUISITIES: Satisfactory score on standardized test or satisfactory completion of other required reading courses.

LEARNING OUTCOMES: In this advanced level reading course students prepare for college-level reading by learning strategies and study skills to help them become more efficient and effective readers. Throughout the course, students will achieve the following learning outcomes

- Demonstrate an improved vocabulary
- Recognize the main idea
- Identify the topic sentence
- Identify supporting details
- Identify the implied main idea
- Recognize patterns of organization
- Detect bias
- Identify logical inferences
- Distinguish between fact and opinion
- Recognize the author's purpose
- Demonstrate improved reading efficiency
- Pass the State Exit Exam

STATE EXIT EXAM: Students in Florida must take the Florida State Exit Exam before exiting this class. In order to pass the exam, students must answer 23 of the 36 questions on the exam correctly. This minimum score must be achieved prior to receiving a grade in this class, regardless of how high you may have scored on class assignments or tests. In other words, you cannot pass this course unless you pass the State Exit Exam.

CLASSROOM ARRANGEMENT AND METHOD OF INSTRUCTION: In this class students will be divided into Cooperative Learning groups. Each group member is asked to participate to the fullest extent on group assignments and projects. Students will receive both

group and individual grades. Additionally, students will receive instruction through lectures, class discussions, peer instruction, audio/video materials, written assignments, and oral reports.

GRADES: Methods used to document a students' mastery of course performance will be teacher observations, classroom assignments, group assignments and examinations. Reading is a skills-based course and a large percentage of class time will be spent practicing the skills introduced and discussed in class. Since much of the course work will be done in class, students need to make an effort to attend every class. Grades for the course will be determined in the following manner:

1. Class Assignments - 25%
2. Vocabulary Tests - 25%
3. Group Assignments -25%
4. Lab Activities - 25%

GRADING SCALE:
90 – 100   A
80 – 89   B
70 – 79   C
Averages below 70 will be recorded as an F

READING LABS: Students will complete a series of lab activities for this class.

IMPORTANT COLLEGE DATES

CALENDAR OF ACTIVITIES

Week	Topic	Activities/Assignments
Week 1	**Course Introduction Chapter 1 The Power of Motivation**	• Interest Inventory • Learning Styles Inventory • Read the chapter on The Power of Motivation • Complete assignments outlined by the instructor • Participate in discussion activities • Complete vocabulary assignments outlined by the instructor • Chapter test • Journal assignment • Group Activity

Week 2	Chapter 2 Active Reading	• Read the chapter on Active Reading • Complete assignments outlined by the instructor • Participate in discussion activities • Complete vocabulary assignments outlined by the instructor • Begin lab assignments outlined by the instructor • Chapter test • Journal assignment • Group Activity
Week 3	Chapter 3 Reading Efficiently	• Read the chapter on Reading Efficiently • Complete assignments outlined by the instructor • Participate in discussion activities • Complete vocabulary assignments outlined by the instructor • Complete lab assignments outlined by the instructor • Chapter test • Journal assignment • Group Activity
Week 4	Chapter 4 Vocabulary Expansion	• Read the chapter on Vocabulary Expansion • Complete assignments outlined by the instructor • Participate in discussion activities • Complete vocabulary assignments outlined by the instructor • Complete lab assignments outlined by the instructor • Chapter test • Journal assignment • Group Activity
Week 5	Chapter 5 Reading for Learning Methods	• Read the chapter on Reading for Learning Methods Complete assignments outlined by the instructor • Participate in discussion activities • Complete vocabulary assignments outlined by the instructor • Complete lab assignments outlined by the instructor • Chapter test • Journal assignment • Group Activity
Week 6	Chapter 6 Main Ideas	• Read the chapter on Main Ideas • Complete assignments outlined by the instructor • Participate in discussion activities • Complete vocabulary assignments outlined by the instructor • Complete lab assignments outlined by the instructor • Journal assignment • Group Activity

Week 7	Chapter 7 Details and Logical Patterns	• Read the chapter on Details and Logical Patterns • Complete assignments outlined by the instructor • Participate in discussion activities • Complete vocabulary assignments outlined by the instructor • Complete lab assignments outlined by the instructor • Journal assignment • Group Activity
Week 8	Chapter 8 Graphic Aids	• Read the chapter on Graphic Aids • Complete assignments outlined by the instructor • Participate in discussion activities • Complete vocabulary assignments outlined by the instructor • Chapter test • Journal assignment • Group Activity
Week 9	Chapter 9 Drawing Conclusions	• Read the chapter on Drawing Conclusions • Complete assignments outlined by the instructor • Participate in discussion activities • Complete vocabulary assignments outlined by the instructor • Chapter test • Journal assignment • Group Activity
Week 10	Chapter 10 Evaluating Argument	• Read the chapter on Evaluating Argument • Complete assignments outlined by the instructor • Participate in discussion activities • Complete vocabulary assignments outlined by the instructor • Complete lab assignments outlined by the instructor • Chapter test • Journal assignment • Group Activity
Week 11	Review Reading and Study Strategies and Test Taking Skills Administer Final Exam	• Review Study Strategies and Test Taking Skills with students • Review materials for final exam • Practice test for the State Exit Exam • Administer State Exit Exam. If you must take a state exit please note that the test contains questions related to the skill areas you have reviewed in this course. The test is timed. • Lab assignments to be completed

Week 12	Final Exam State Exit Exam Student-Teacher Conferences	• Administer final exam • If you did not pass the State Exit Exam, you will be given another chance to take a different form of the same test. Please talk with your instructor to schedule a time to come in and take the exam. • Participate in a student-teacher conference about the course

SAMPLE 16-WEEK SYLLABUS

Term/Year:	
Reference Number:	
Instructor:	
Office:	
E-mail:	
Phone Number:	
Web Page:	
Classroom:	

REQUIRED TEXTBOOK:
Empowered College Reading by Linda Lee

COURSE DESCRIPTION: This reading course is designed to enhance basic reading skills, develop higher-level vocabulary and comprehension skills, textbook reading techniques, and learning strategies needed for success in college. Students must satisfy appropriate exit level scores in addition to the coursework in order to complete this course successfully.

COURSE PREREQUISITIES: Satisfactory score on standardized test or satisfactory completion of other required reading courses.

LEARNING OUTCOMES: In this advanced level reading course students prepare for college-level reading by learning strategies and study skills to help them become more efficient and effective readers. Throughout the course, students will achieve the following learning outcomes

- Demonstrate an improved vocabulary
- Recognize the main idea
- Identify the topic sentence
- Identify supporting details
- Identify the implied main idea
- Recognize patterns of organization
- Detect bias
- Identify logical inferences
- Distinguish between fact and opinion
- Recognize the author's purpose
- Demonstrate improved reading efficiency
- Pass the State Exit Exam

STATE EXIT EXAM: Students in Florida must take the Florida State Exit Exam before exiting this class. In order to pass the exam, students must answer 23 of the 36 questions on the exam correctly. This minimum score must be achieved prior to receiving a grade in this class, regardless of how high you may have scored on class assignments or tests. In other words, you cannot pass this course unless you pass the State Exit Exam.

CLASSROOM ARRANGEMENT AND METHOD OF INSTRUCTION: In this class students will be divided into Cooperative Learning groups. Each group member is asked to participate to the fullest extent on group assignments and projects. Students will receive both

group and individual grades. Additionally, students will receive instruction through lectures, class discussions, peer instruction, audio/video materials, written assignments, and oral reports.

GRADES: Methods used to document a students' mastery of course performance will be teacher observations, classroom assignments, group assignments and examinations. Reading is a skills-based course and a large percentage of class time will be spent practicing the skills introduced and discussed in class. Since much of the course work will be done in class, students need to make an effort to attend every class. Grades for the course will be determined in the following manner:

1. Class Assignments - 25%
2. Vocabulary Tests - 25%
3. Group Assignments -25%
4. Lab Activities - 25%

GRADING SCALE:
90 – 100   A
80 – 89   B
70 – 79   C
Averages below 70 will be recorded as an F

READING LABS: Students will complete a series of lab activities for this class. Lab folders must be completed and turned in on the due date assigned by the instructor. Lab folders not turned in on time or incomplete will receive a 0 grade.

IMPORTANT COLLEGE DATES

CALENDAR OF ACTIVITIES

Week	Topic	Activities/Assignments
Week 1	**Course Introduction; Student Introduction**	• Diagnostic Pre-test • Interest Inventory • Learning Styles Inventory • Team Project
Week 2	**Chapter 1 The Power of Motivation**	• Read the chapter on The Power of Motivation • Complete assignments outlined by the instructor • Participate in discussion activities

		• Complete vocabulary assignments outlined by the instructor. • Complete lab assignments outlined by the instructor • Chapter test • Journal assignment • Group Activity
Week 3	**Chapter 2** **Active Reading**	• Read the chapter on Active Reading • Complete assignments outlined by the instructor • Participate in discussion activities • Complete vocabulary assignments outlined by the instructor • Complete lab assignments outlined by the instructor • Chapter test • Journal assignment • Group Activity
Week 4	**Chapter 3** **Reading Efficiently**	• Read the chapter on Reading Efficiently • Complete assignments outlined by the instructor • Participate in discussion activities • Complete vocabulary assignments outlined by the instructor • Complete lab assignments outlined by the instructor • Chapter test • Journal assignment • Group Activity
Week 5	**Chapter 4** **Vocabulary Expansion**	• Read the chapter on Vocabulary Expansion • Complete assignments outlined by the instructor • Participate in discussion activities • Complete vocabulary assignments outlined by the instructor • Complete lab assignments outlined by the instructor • Chapter test • Journal assignment • Group Activity
Week 6	**Chapter 5** **Reading for Learning Methods**	• Read the chapter on Reading for Learning Methods Complete assignments outlined by the instructor • Participate in discussion activities • Complete vocabulary assignments outlined by the instructor • Complete lab assignments outlined by the instructor • Chapter test • Journal assignment • Group Activity

Week 7	**Chapter 6** **Main Ideas**	• Read the chapter on Main Ideas • Complete assignments outlined by the instructor • Participate in discussion activities • Complete vocabulary assignments outlined by the instructor • Complete lab assignments outlined by the instructor • Journal assignment • Group Activity
Week 8	**Continue Chapter 6** **Main Ideas**	• Review the chapter on Main Ideas • Complete assignments outlined by the instructor • Participate in discussion activities • Complete vocabulary assignments outlined by the instructor • Complete lab assignments outlined by the instructor • Chapter test • Journal assignment • Group Activity
Week 9	**Chapter 7** **Details and Logical** **Patterns**	• Read the chapter on Details and Logical Patterns • Complete assignments outlined by the instructor • Participate in discussion activities • Complete vocabulary assignments outlined by the instructor • Complete lab assignments outlined by the instructor • Journal assignment • Group Activity
Week 10	**Continue Chapter 7** **Details and Logical** **Patterns**	• Review the chapter on Details and Logical Patterns • Complete assignments outlined by the instructor • Participate in discussion activities • Complete vocabulary assignments outlined by the instructor • Complete lab assignments outlined by the instructor • Chapter test • Journal assignment • Group Activity
Week 11	**Chapter 8** **Graphic Aids**	• Read the chapter on Graphic Aids • Complete assignments outlined by the instructor • Participate in discussion activities • Complete vocabulary assignments outlined by the instructor • Chapter test • Journal assignment • Group Activity

Week 12	Chapter 9 Drawing Conclusions	• Read the chapter on Drawing Conclusions • Complete assignments outlined by the instructor • Participate in discussion activities • Complete vocabulary assignments outlined by the instructor • Chapter test • Journal assignment • Group Activity
Week 13	Chapter 10 Evaluating Argument	• Read the chapter on Evaluating Argument • Complete assignments outlined by the instructor • Participate in discussion activities • Complete vocabulary assignments outlined by the instructor • Complete lab assignments outlined by the instructor • Chapter test • Journal assignment • Group Activity
Week 14	Review Reading and Study Strategies and Test Taking Skills	• Review Study Strategies and Test Taking Skills with students • Complete assignments outlined by the instructor • Participate in discussion activities • Complete vocabulary assignments outlined by the instructor • Complete lab assignments outlined by the instructor • Review materials for final exam • Practice test for the State Exit Exam
Week 15	Final Exam State Exit Exam	• Administer final exam • Administer state exit exam. If you must take a state exit please note that the test contains questions related to the skill areas you have reviewed in this course. The test is timed. • Lab assignments to be completed
Week 16	Retake State Exit Exam Student-Teacher Conferences	• If you did not pass the State Exit Exam, you will be given another chance to take a different form of the same test. Please talk with your instructor to schedule a time to come in and take the exam. • Participate in a student-teacher conference about the course

Chapter One: The Power of Motivation

Summary

Motivation is a life changing factor that can enable you to be successful in college, and it can help you generate energy to keep you focused on your classes. You must create your own motivation to meet the challenges presented in your college classes. It is not the teacher's responsibility to make you do your work; it is your responsibility.

College classes will challenge you to use your mind in new ways, to expand your skills, and to add to your current knowledge base. You need to create your own energy and interest in order to succeed in your college classes.

Motivation and ability work hand in hand to help you perform in college. If you are highly motivated, it can change your performance even when your ability levels are low. Reading involves various processes and skills. It is important to begin each task by assessing your ability levels and by predicting your comprehension. You can modify your comprehension prediction and use additional sources as you complete the task. The methods you chose to use and your motivational levels will help you deal with the challenges you will face academically. Think of each task with a positive "can do" attitude, use positive self talk to create interest, and think of techniques to use that will enable you to be successful.

There are four stages of motivation to use to attack your reading tasks. First, you must find a way to become interested in your task, preview the task, plan how to divide the task into manageable sections, think how the accomplishment will help you, and set motivating goals to complete. Second, concentrate your energy on the task by thinking positively and using methods that will help you succeed. Make sure you manage your time wisely. The third step is to evaluate your progress as you go through the task and make sure to give yourself feedback about your behavior. Maintain an internal locus of control, which means you know that you are in control of your performance, and believe in your ability to complete the task. Use positive visualizations, think optimistically about your abilities, and manage your stress by creating balance in your life, controlling the number of activities you do outside of school, prioritize your tasks, find others to help you with encouragement, view problems as challenges with solutions, and control you attitudes about your grades. The last stage is to think about your achievements and reward yourself with extrinsic rewards, tangibles, or intrinsic rewards that are pleasurable thoughts about your success. Look at the information from the task again and review it independently or with others, think how the new knowledge can help you in your life or in other classes, and reward yourself.

Teaching Tips:

- As an introduction to the unit have the students think of an activity they can do outstandingly. Have them write the techniques they used to learn how to do it. How did motivation play a part in this process? What rewards did they receive?

- After you have talked about motivation and the ideas in the chapter, have the students consider if the extrinsic rewards, or tangible rewards, motivate you more or less than the intrinsic rewards, or feelings of satisfaction?

Suggested Activities:

- Ask every other row of students to turn to their left or right and to create a list of five ways to motivate yourself to read a chapter about a subject in which you have no interest. Give the students 3-5 minutes to complete the activity. The sharing activity can be completed as a class discussion with each group sharing their lists or by having the teacher compile the lists into one list.

- Write a journal entry explaining how teachers in your life have used intrinsic and extrinsic rewards with students in their classes. Give specific examples of the rewards. Have the students state whether the type of reward was effective. How did teachers help students to create intrinsic rewards for themselves?

- Have students create an intrinsic and extrinsic reward list. Have them try to consider when each reward would be appropriate.

- Have the class form groups of three. Tell the groups to create a script using positive self-talk to prepare themselves to take a final in one of their college classes.

The Power of Motivation Test 1

1. Whose job is it to provide lasting motivation for you?

    a. your teachers
    b. your friends
    c. yourself
    d. your professor

2. According to the author, one of the forces that can be life altering is

    a. energy.
    b. engagement.
    c. interest.
    d. motivation.

3. The four stages of academic motivation are

    a. engage your interest, focus your efforts, monitor your progress, and reflect on your gains.
    b. be positive you can do well, do your assignments, go to class, and use good time management.
    c. decide what needs to be done, engage your interest, and do the work.
    d. focus your efforts, find problems, solve them, and move to the next topic.

4. Negative self talk should

    a. be replaced by the positive self affirmation, "I can do it."
    b. be replaced with a comment about an interesting part of the reading.
    c. be replaced with a comment that states your goal and your method to achieve it.
    d. be allowed for a short time because a little apprehension can be motivating to many people.

5. Which two students would most likely get the highest grade?

        1. a student with high motivation and low ability
        2. a student with low motivation and low ability
        3. a student with high motivation and high ability
        4. a student with low motivation and high ability

    a. 1 and 2
    b. 3 and 4
    c. 1 and 3
    d. 2 and 4

6. Techniques that can help you to become engaged are all of the following except

    a. survey the task to see what is required and to think about what you know about the topic.
    b. talk with people involved with the task and ask why they are interested in completing the task or learning the material.
    c. divide the task with others to quickly complete the task.
    d. create personal goals that make you want to complete the task or tasks.

7. Which of the following steps from the list will help the learner make the motivating goals personal?

        1. Use the words "I want."
        2. Make the task to achieve specific, so you know what you will need to do.
        3. Make the topic on which you will focus precise.
        4. Include a reason why finishing this task will benefit you.
        5. Include a bonus reward which states something you will do for yourself as a reward.

    a. 1, 3, and 5
    b. 2 and 4
    c. 2, 3, and 4
    d. 1, 2, 3, 4, and 5

8. When you are distracted by thoughts while you are working, you should

    a. ignore them because you must stay focused.
    b. write the concerns down, so you can think about them later.
    c. do the action and then return immediately, then return to your college work.
    d. write out a specific plan to deal with them later.

9. Which statement is true?

    a. Cramming works for most college exams.
    b. Do one week's class work for each class during one work session.
    c. College needs to take a high priority in your life.
    d. The kitchen table is a great place to do homework.

10. When you have an internal locus of control, you might say

    a. "I am not smart enough."
    b. "I have been successful in this subject before, so I can do this if I have a plan."
    c. "The teacher did not cover the information thoroughly enough, so I did not pass."
    d. "Nothing I could have done would have changed the outcome."

11. A mental rehearsal of a skill or experience is called a

    a. visualization.
    b. self-fulfilling prophecy.
    c. cerebral prophecy.
    d. psychological practice.

12. Having average motivation can

    a. give you a clear message that you are on track.
    b. indicate that you must make changes.
    c. offer clear guidelines about what you need to do.
    d. not be very useful.

13. According to Oprah Winfrey, we are always one choice away from

    a. failure as a student.
    b. success as a student.
    c. a new beginning.
    d. becoming what we dream about.

14. Ability includes

    a. performance and success in your academic life.
    b. knowledge and skills you currently possess.
    c. the desire and energy to achieve.
    d. the power that drives us each day.

15. Students with an external locus of control will

    a. believe their effort and learning affect their college success more than natural ability.
    b. are optimists and believe they can do almost anything if they try.
    c. are pessimistic.
    d. get higher grades.

The Power of Motivation Test 2

1. Monitoring your academic progress is important in college because

    a. it affects your motivation and sense of control.
    b. you need to withdraw from courses you will not pass.
    c. you need feedback from your professors.
    d. it affects your external locus of control.

2. To help your stress management, you should

    a. always strive for the highest grades.
    b. take many courses, so you can finish college early.
    c. develop support groups.
    d. all of the above.

3. During which stage of motivation does a student develop the "I achieved something" attitude?

    a. monitor progress
    b. focus efforts
    c. reflect on gains
    d. engage interest

4. Balancing your life in college is important because

    a. you need a healthy routine.
    b. you need rest.
    c. you need to speak and work with others.
    d. all of the above

5. Which statement is false?

    a. It is important to set limits on non-school activities.
    b. It is important to prioritize your chores and assignments.
    c. It is important to develop support groups in college, so you can make new friends.
    d. It is important to take a problem solving approach to course information difficulties.

6. An example of an intrinsic reward is

    a. receiving good grades.
    b. attending a play you want to see as a reward for getting your work completed on time.
    c. eating a food you like because you completed your project.
    d. praising yourself after you complete your project.

7. Which statement is true?

    a. Self-motivation can be developed by anyone.
    b. The best motivational sources are your professors.
    c. The best motivational sources are your family and friends.
    d. Motivation uses up your mental fuel.

8. Assessing your motivational level and ability levels for a particular subject can help you predict

    a. your comprehension level and the academic adjustments you will need to make.
    b. whether you will need an intrinsic or extrinsic reward to complete the task.
    c. what kinds of visualizations to create.
    d. the objectives for the class.

9. According to the author, the best reward for true motivation would be

    a. a snack.
    b. a good grade.
    c. the feeling of pride you get from a job well done.
    d. a leisurely activity at the end of a project you have completed.

10. Which techniques would not solidify your accomplishment?

    a. Set limits on school activities.
    b. Reward yourself often.
    c. Recognize what is useful.
    d. Review the information.

11. When you have problems becoming interested in the material, you should

    a. force yourself to do it.
    b. try to become intellectually involved.
    c. tell yourself you are worthless if you do not complete this task.
    d. jump right into the material.

12. According to Francie Larrieu Smith, the most important thing about motivation is

    a. your ability.
    b. your attitude.
    c. goal setting.
    d. random work.

13. According to the author, one of the reasons many athletes are successful is

    a. due to threats from their coaches.
    b. because they receive many tangible rewards.
    c. due to their whole-hearted participation.
    d. because the team works together.

14. An example of positive self-talk is

    a. "The other people in my class distract me, so I cannot listen."
    b. "I am positive I cannot do this math."
    c. "The instructor gives me bad grades because she likes men better than women."
    d. "I can learn what I need to know if I study."

15. Visualizations are

    a. pictures from your text.
    b. movies teachers show.
    c. mental rehearsals.
    d. your knowledge and skills.

Answer Key Test 1

1. c
2. d
3. a
4. c
5. c
6. c
7. d
8. b
9. c
10. b
11. a
12. d
13. c
14. b
15. c

Answer Key Test 2

1. a
2. c
3. c
4. d
5. c
6. d
7. a
8. a
9. c
10. a
11. b
12. c
13. c
14. d
15. c

Chapter Two: Active Reading

Summary

To read college materials effectively, you must use strategies that help you comprehend the author's ideas and identify the material you will need for completing tasks in the future. Since the goal of college reading is to learn, it is extremely important to become an active reader. Becoming an active reader will help you to competently and accurately handle academically difficult, complex, and technical college texts and will help you to figure out how and when the presented information will help you in the future.

Active readers approach material in a positive, motivated manner with an effective plan for reading that evaluates their prior knowledge and incorporates methods that increase comprehension and enhance memory. Active readers make the choice to create their own interest and to stay involved. Passive readers rely on the author to stimulate their interest, use the author's words to study, and do not work to keep involved in the material they are reading.

To read an essay actively, you must first preread the title, the introduction, the summary or conclusion, and the first sentence of major paragraphs. Next, you must question and react to the author's ideas in order to create interest in the material. The next step is to mentally divide the material into sections by using the major paragraphs to guide you, and then create a purpose for reading each section by asking yourself what you instructor would want you to know about the section. In addition, you should consider how the information could help you in your life or your class.

During the reading of the essay, it is important to develop questions about the material you have read by turning the title and key words into questions using the words what, why, and how or by asking broad questions. As you read, you should try to find the answers to your questions. Identify the important information and record the information by underlining key ideas and making margin notes that include labels, notes, personal reactions, and comments. Pay attention to your level of understanding and identify areas in which you have problems.

As you are reading, pay attention to the problem areas where you have difficulty understanding. Try to figure out what the text means by saying the information in your own words. When there are groups of related paragraphs, try to work out the relationships between the ideas. Make notations in the margin and try to create sentences from your margin notes. Take time to recite the information and reflect about the ideas before you stop your work.

During the reading of a textbook chapter, most of the steps of PDQ3R are the same, but a few of the steps have additional steps. When you preread the chapter, you read the introduction, the summary or conclusion, and the first sentence of the major paragraphs in the body. You should also look at the boldfaced or italicized headings and the graphics. When you divide the chapter, use the headings to help you split the chapter up into manageable parts. Outline the important ideas in the chapter and create a map to show the organization of the ideas. Use your prior knowledge and ability to concentrate to help you decide on the divisions to use for your chapter. Use the headings to create the questions to help create interest and to guide your reading. Write your question in the margins next to the paragraphs that might answer the questions. As you read, underline the pertinent information and record the answers to the questions. As you reflect and recite, add reactions and comments to your margin notes.

When you have finished reading, reward yourself for completing the task, and then plan how you will review the information. Answer the questions you wrote, create notes or flashcards, and make other learning tools. Discussing the ideas with others is also an effective review method.

Teaching Tips:

- Model how you would apply this method to an essay. Explain each step as you do it.

- Model the techniques for using this method with a chapter. Go through a step-by-step explanation of how you would preread, divide, and question for a chapter.

Suggested Activities:

- How would you vary the study method for reading for fun? Reading an article to figure out if you would use it for research paper, reading an article for a class assignment but not the final, or reading material you wish to learn for your own information?

- Have each student pair with another student. Assign a chapter to read. Have the first student go through the chapter and read the parts of the chapter he or she would preread to the second student. Have the second student state how they would divide the chapter into manageable parts. Have each student create 5-10 questions about the chapter.

- Have students write out how they would complete each part of PDQ3R with an assignment in another class or with an article you provide.

- After reading a reading or chapter, assign pairs of students to mark the chapter and to make margin notes. After they have finished, have the students create notes or other learning tools to use to record, organize, and remember the information.

- Ask the students to imagine they were in an American History in the 19th and 20th Century class. Then have the students write a journal entry that explains how they would find information that could help them figure out what life was like in the early 1900s.

Active Reading Test 1

1. As you do close reading, you should do the following activities

   a. highlight the sentences as you read, make sure you have a purpose for reading, and copy the boldfaced and italicized text to use as notes when you study.
   b. think of questions you prepared during your prereading, read to locate the answers to your questions, mark the text, and write notes in the margins.
   c. look for the boldfaced and italicized parts, underline important sentences, and make flash cards.
   d. create question about the material you are reading, write the questions in the margin, and highlight the answers in the text.

2. Margin notes should include

   a. short notes that condense intricate ideas.
   b. labels about the important types of information.
   c. the reader's reactions, reflections, and ideas about the material.
   d. all of the above

3. Readers should recite in order to

    a. review the boldfaced print and write down the important information.
    b. check and improve their comprehension of groups of paragraphs.
    c. memorize the information from the text.
    d. all of the above

4. To read the textbook chapter actively

    a. first preread the various chapter sections, divide the chapters by topics or sections, and create goals for each of the reading sections.
    b. first create questions, then read to find the answers, and then write notes.
    c. first create goals for each reading task, read, and then divide the information to making taking notes easier.
    d. first divide the chapter into sections, read, and then answer questions the author has written.

5. It is necessary to plan strategies for your reading for college because

    a. your reading is the first step in your college classes that leads to success with work tasks such as exam preparation, studying, and writing activities.
    b. many college classes often have larger and more challenging work loads than most high school classes.
    c. any material you may miss in your reading may have an effect on the other work for the class.
    d. all of the above

6. Characteristics of passive readers include

    a. mental engagement.
    b. interest.
    c. high stress.
    d. the selection and use of methods that get the reader involved with the text.

7. The best way to read a college text is to

    a. look up the assignment, open the book to the correct page, and read the pages assigned.
    b. preread the assigned pages, divide the assignment into logical units of study, make up questions, read, identify the important information while noting problem areas, and go over the material after reading.
    c. preread the assignment, create questions you hope the author will answer, read the pages assigned, and highlight the important information you think you will need to know the class.
    d. look up the assignment, divide the assignment into logical units of study, read the pages assigned, answer the author's questions, and highlight the important information you think you will need to know for the assignments and tests

8. Active readers

    a. read one sentence after another, reread, relocate, and recomprehend the information at a later time.
    b. get overly focused on separate words or sentences.
    c. think how the pieces of information fit together and check for problem areas.
    d. jump right into their reading by reading the assignment straight through.

9. Preread to

   a. find the topics covered and the answers to the chapter's questions.
   b. identify the topic, start to think, and get motivated.
   c. find out what new vocabulary will be covered and then use your dictionary to locate the meanings of the words.
   d. find the answers to the author's questions or the teacher's study guide.

10. When you preread and work on the second step of PDQ3R, you should

    a. find how the material is organized in order to have more efficient and accurate comprehension.
    b. divide the material by the location of the author's questions, so you can deduce the answers to the author's questions quickly.
    c. decode the new words by dividing the larger words into the prefixes, suffixes, and roots.
    d. deduce quiz questions by changing titles into questions by adding the question words who, what, when, where, why, and how.

11. Complete step 2 of PDQ3R by writing

    a. each new word with its definition.
    b. your motivational goal starting with "I want" and including your objective.
    c. the quiz questions you have created.
    d. the answers to the author's questions or the teacher's questions.

12. PDQ3R, an effective study strategy, stands for

    a. preread assignment, divide, question, recite, recall, and review.
    b. preread assignment, decode, quiz yourself, read, recall, and review.
    c. preread assignment, deduce, quiz yourself, recite, recall, and review.
    d. preread assignment, divide, question, read, recite, and review.

13. When is the best time for active readers to review the material the first time?

    a. the night before the exam
    b. the week before the exam
    c. soon after you read the material
    d. after you have completed all the assignments related to the chapter

14. Which description describes an active reader?

    a. John goes home after each class, opens his book to the correct page, reads until the end of the assignment, and then closes his book. He feels great because he has done his assignment.
    b. The night before class Jasmine opens her book to the correct page, looks at the pictures and headings and thinks about the subject. She remembers her seventh grade teacher lecturing about the topic and guesses that there will be some similarities. The next morning she reads the assignment and makes marks in the margins about the subject and relationships to her life.
    c. Jennifer waits until two hours before class to work on her assignment. She opens the book, looks at the pictures, the title, the introduction and the summary. She reads the questions and thinks she might know the answers, so she closes the book and hurries to class.

d. Joaquin goes to the library after class where he sits at a computer. He looks up his text's website and accesses the student site where he copies the study guide for the chapter the teacher assigned. He looks up the answers to the questions and rewrites the part of the text that answered the questions. Then he closes the book and puts it into his bag until he goes to class.

15. Passive readers

    a. expect the author to catch their interest.
    b. question what they read.
    c. relate what they read to their own lives.
    d. are emotional about what they read.

Active Reading Test 2

1. Prereading and dividing the material you are to read will help you to

    a. find the parts you can skip.
    b. reduce your assignment.
    c. engage interest.
    d. help you find the answers to the questions without reading the text.

2. Preread by reading

    a. The title first, the introduction second, the conclusion third, and the first sentence of the major or longest paragraphs last.
    b. the first sentence of the major or longest paragraphs first, the conclusion second, the title third, and the introduction last.
    c. the conclusion first, the first sentence of the major or longest paragraphs second, the title third, and the introduction last.
    d. the title first, the first sentence of the major or longest paragraphs second, the conclusion third, and the introduction last.

3. Prereading includes

    a. marking the test.
    b. reacting to the author's point.
    c. reciting the important points of the reading.
    d. writing the important points of the reading.

4. Your comprehension of the text will be faster and more accurate if you

    a. read the chapter and reread it the night before the exam.
    b. divide the chapter into five page sections and read them separately.
    c. read the chapter and write all the boldfaced information as your notes.
    d. create a mental road map of the chapter.

5. Active readers pause from time to time while they are reading

    a. think how the pieces of information fit together.
    b. recite the information and to make sure they understand the information.
    c. check for reading problems.
    d. all of the above

6. The three objectives to dividing textbook chapters are

    a. to split the reading into easy sections you can read at different times, answer the questions the author has included, and write notes for each section of the chapter.
    b. to count the number of pages, to divide by four to obtain the number of pages in each section, and then to create questions to go with each section.
    c. to understand how the author has organized the information, to split the reading into easily managed tasks, and to create goals for each reading task.
    d. to look at the boldfaced heading, divide the sections by where the largest headings are located, and to create visualizations to go with each section.

7. Make a map of the chapter headings in order to

    a. recite the information from the chapter.
    b. decide what information you can skip.
    c. create a set of notes to use study.
    d. to help you understand how the author has organized the material.

8. Two things to consider as you plan how to divide and read the chapter are

    a. your prior knowledge (what you already know about the subject) and the length of time you can focus.
    b. the amount of time you have to study and the length of time you can concentrate.
    c. your background knowledge and the amount of time you have to study.
    d. the length of time you can concentrate and the length of time you can study.

9. To mark texts you must

    1. underline the key words.
    2. highlight important sentences.
    3. create margin notes that include useful questions.
    4. create margin notes that include your reactions.

    a. 1 and 2
    b. 1, 2, and 3
    c. 1 and 3
    d. 1, 3, and 4

10. Maps are a helpful way to study because

    a. the ideas are presented in a manner that shows the organization as well as important ideas.
    b. the author's words are used to create the maps, so you can recognize the ideas on the quizzes.
    c. they can show the reader information about location.
    d. they have a legend to help students understand what each symbol represents.

11. Reading material about interesting new subjects that you have not learned about before

    a. will be motivating and therefore easier.
    b. can be easy if you read the new vocabulary first.
    c. may be challenging because you do not have background knowledge.
    d. can be challenging, but because it is new information it should be easier to focus your attention.

12. Comprehension includes

    1. reading the words.
    2. thinking.
    3. combining textbook information with your vocabulary.
    4. combining textbook information with your background knowledge.

    a. 1, 2, and 4
    b. 1, 2, 3, and 4
    c. 1, 2, and 3
    d. 1 and 2

13. Which one of these rewards, according to the author, does not result from participating in class?

    a. praise
    b. improved concentration
    c. understanding
    d. friendship

14. To divide an essay, you should

    a. count to pages in the essay and divide by four.
    b. look at the body of the essay and count the number of major or long body paragraphs.
    c. divide the essay into the introduction, the body, and the summary.
    d. since essays are short, divide it in half.

15. As part of the divide step of PDQ3R you should

    a. identify what you can personally gain from the information.
    b. highlight the important parts of each section.
    c. answer the author's questions.
    d. recreate the graphics in the text.

Answer Key Test 1

1. b
2. d
3. b
4. b
5. d
6. c
7. b
8. c
9. b

10. a
11. b
12. d
13. c
14. b
15. a

Answer Key Test 2

1.   c
2.   a
3.   b
4.   d
5.   d
6.   c
7.   c
8.   a
9.   d
10. a
11. c
12. b
13. d
14. b
15. a

Chapter Three: Reading Efficiently

Summary

Reading rate and speed are both important factors in improving reading efficiency. Factors involved in improving rate and speed require a reader to keep his or her mind focused on the reading material, comprehend the information within the materials, and continue to move forward through the material. These factors, coupled with being able to read at varying or flexible speeds, are important in terms of how efficiently one reads. Reading at varying speeds is a key element in getting through lengthy assignments with a degree of comprehension needed to master course objectives.

To develop an efficient style of reading, it is imperative to know how to choose efficient rates and identify personal speed blocks. To determine the best speed for reading materials, think about the purpose for which you are reading. Understanding your purpose for reading has to do with how important the information is, what you will do with it in the future, and how much you already know. After you have established your purpose for reading, then assess the difficulty of the text. For example, if your purpose for reading requires learning and the text is difficult, read at a slower pace to give yourself a chance to absorb the material. If you are preparing to survey the reading materials and the text is easy to read, use a faster pace.

To help determine the most efficient rate for reading materials you need to recognize self-restricting ideas and habits, or blocks, that promote speeds that are too fast or too slow. These blocks may be psychological, physical, or skill based.

Psychological blocks can include lack of motivation and misconceptions about reading. Efficient reading requires high motivation at each stage. If you are not engaged, you won't have the desire to read the texts you dread and see it as boring. Physical blocks can include eye strain and the way you move your eyes and focus on a page. For example, poor line tracking–when your eyes do not stay on the right line, over-fixating–staring at the text much longer than necessary,–and regression–looking back at what you have already read. Skill based blocks can include weaknesses in vocabulary and comprehension and the use of passive reading approaches.

Techniques that can help eliminate some of these blocks can greatly improve reading efficiency. Psychological blocks can be eliminated by taking control of your reading and using motivation techniques and new ideas to help clear up misconceptions. Physical blocks can be eliminated by physically changing your body position when you read and working to overcome inefficient eye movements. Eye movements can be improved with line focusing and eye swing exercises, as well as pacing methods. Skill based blocks, also referred to as method blocks, can be eliminated by using active reading techniques and phrase reading (reading groups of words or more than one word at a time). Additionally, use skimming and scanning techniques whenever your purpose for reading is to review or locate information.

Teaching Tips:

- Encourage to students to practice increasing their eye span. Explain how taking in larger word groups can help them improve their reading rate.

- Encourage students to use their finger, pen, or pencil as a guide to pace themselves as they read.

- Try and help students break the habit of regressing when they read.

- Review the SQ3R study system with students and explain how it can help them learn to read more efficiently and effectively recall pertinent information that may be included on exams. Explain that the acronym, SQ3R, stands for the five steps included in the study system: survey, question, read, recite, and review.

- Use the three-step process below to help students build their reading rate, speed and comprehension:

STEP ONE

<u>Prereading</u>

1. Make use of prior knowledge.

If you are reading a textbook, an informative book chapter, or an expository article, read the parts of the chapter listed below first. Make sure you locate the new vocabulary and find the meanings. You can do this by using context clues, dividing the word into word parts and thinking about their meanings in relationship to the reading's subject, or looking in another source. As you are reading the sections, ask yourself the following question.

What do I already know about this?

This will help to stimulate your memory, and it will help prepare you to read effectively.

Look at how the information is organized within the chapter because it will help you organize the information when you wish to study.

<u>Chapter</u>

Title	boldfaced & italicized words
pictures/diagrams/captions	numbered/bulleted items
introduction/first paragraph	summary
subtitles	questions

As you preread a story, read the following parts and try to create a picture of the setting and the characters in your mind. When you visualize, it prepares you to create a picture in which the story will take place. If you try to create the picture for the story as you go along, you find a need to make changes and then you lose some of the details.

<u>Story</u>

title	when
pictures	where
introductory paragraph	last paragraph
who/what	questions

2. Question yourself.

Ask yourself, "What will I need to know about this material?" This will help you to focus on your reading, to remember what we read, and to create a method to decide what will be important. Create focus questions about the subject or use the author's questions to help you concentrate on the material.

You can predict the information you will need to know by thinking of test questions your professor might ask about the material. You can do this because you have taken many tests throughout your educational experiences, and you can predict the types of questions professors will ask. Professors will often ask for you to put different points of information together in order to answer some of their questions, but if you have the basic knowledge in your memory banks, you should be able to do this.

Prereading has an additional advantage. Because your brain is prepared, it can process the information you are reading more readily. Therefore, you may find your reading rate will increase, but your understanding will be accurate.

STEP TWO

Reading Effectively

Good readers do not read everything at the same speed. You must slow down when you get to unfamiliar material or complicated ideas. You can speed up when the material in the reading is information you already know.

Use *metacognitive* strategies by paying attention to the material you are reading and check your understanding by stating the information in your own words.

Connect the new knowledge to your old knowledge by using various methods. Plan methods to help you remember the information.

1. Predict what the author will write about the subject.

Predict what you think the reading will state by using your prior knowledge about the subject or similar subjects. Read the material to see if you were right or wrong. Adjust your ideas if you need to do so.

2. Picture or diagram the material.

Color can be used to differentiate specific information or the importance level of the information. An example would be to use color on a picture of the human body to show which parts of the body work in which systems. The circulatory system could be red and the respiratory system could be blue.

3. Associate.

Relate new material to old (the relationship may be strange, but if it makes sense to you, it might work). The strange and funny analogies are often the ones you remember the most readily. Research has shown that associations are easier to remember if there is an emotion associated to it.

4. Stop occasionally and try to paraphrase the material.

If you can repeat the ideas in your own words, it will assure you that you understand the material. Your brain will also process the material more easily if it is in words *with which you are familiar.*

5. Find the confusing points. Figure out strategies to use to solve the problems.

Figure out a method to make the points less confusing.
Ask your teacher, or a friend, for additional information.
Look for material about the subject in a book or on the Web. (Make sure your Web sources are accurate).

STEP THREE

Postreading

1. Plan to review within 24 hours!

Studies have shown we forget information quickly after the 24-hour period has passed. Recent studies have suggested that less than 12 hours is even better. You do not have to take intensive notes, but you do need to go over the material in your own words.

2. Vary methods to study and review.

Do something with the material that will get you involved with it. Do not use the author's words. Highlighting is a good start, but then write the important ideas in your own words in the margins. Label points and write the types of relationships between the points. Number ideas that are listed. It makes studying easier if you know how many items need to be remembered. Create acronyms with the first letters of the items in the lists.

Use note-taking, outlining, summarizing, mapping, annotating, stating the information to a friend or a tape recorder, or paraphrasing. Create songs and raps. Type or rewrite the information in your own words. Use methods that work with your learning style. Use flash cards.

3. Repeat the important information in your own words unless a term is technical.

4. Review the information often.

This may seem like it would take a long time, but as you go over the information you will find that it takes less and less time each time you study. It is important to review from time to time even when it feels like you know the material. The more you study, the more likely it is that you will retain the material for a longer period of time.

Suggested Activities:

- Set aside some time in class to have students read passages of varying lengths. Time students at different intervals (1 minute, 3 minutes, 5 minutes). Help them monitor their progress by calculating the number of words they are reading per minute.

- Type sentences on a sheet of paper using various point sizes. Have students use the sheet to practice increasing their eye spans.

- Have students pair up and ask them to take turns watching each other read a short passage. Ask them to make notations about what they observe in terms of their partner's eye movements. Give them time to discuss their observations with one another.

- Using the information included in the teaching tips above, have students complete the following activity.

1. What are the five steps to the SQ3R study strategy?

    a._____

    b._____

    c._____

    d._____

    e._____

2. Why should you use a study system?

_____

_____

3. How soon should you review the new knowledge?

_____

4. What should you do <u>as you read</u> to help retain the knowledge?

    a. _____

    b. _____

    c. _____

Reading Efficiency Test 1

Fill in the missing information for the questions below:

1. Factors involved in improving rate and speed require a reader to keep his or her mind

  1.

  2.

  3.

2. A key element in getting through lengthy assignments is _____

_____.

3. One way to determine the best speed for reading materials is _____

_____.

4. To help determine the most efficient rate for reading materials you need to _____

_____.

5. It is important to understand when these habits or blocks are _____

_____.

6. These blocks may be _____, _____, and _____.

7. Psychological blocks can include a lack of _____ and _____

_____.

8. Some examples of physical blocks are _____, _____,

and _____.

9. Physical blocks can be eliminated by _____

and _____.

10. Skill based blocks can include _____

and _____.

Match the following terms to the correct definition:

_____1. skimming and scanning   a. looking back at what you have already read
_____2. poor line tracking   b. staring at the test much longer than necessary
_____3. eye movements   c. when your eyes do not stay on the right line
_____4. over-fixating   d. techniques used when your purpose for reading
                                          is to review or locate information
_____5. regression   e. can be improved with line focusing and eye
                                          swing exercises

Reading Efficiency Test 2

_____1. efficient rates exercises   a. can be improved with line focusing and eye
                                              swing
_____2. skimming and scanning   b. looking back at what you have already read
_____2. poor line tracking   c. weaknesses in vocabulary and comprehension
                                              and the use of passive reading approaches
_____3. eye movements   d. when your eyes do not stay on the right line
_____4. psychological blocks   e. poor line tracking, over-fixating, and regression
_____5. regression   f. optimum speed choice determined by a reader's
                                              purpose and the difficulty of the text
_____6. over-fixating   g. motivation and misconceptions about reading
_____7. physical blocks to review or locate   h. techniques used when your purpose for reading
        information   is
_____8. skill based blocks necessary   i. much longer than staring at the test
_____9. speed and efficiency   j. essential when you are reading for learning
_____10. flexible reading   k. reading at a pace that keeps the mind focused

Fill in the missing information for the questions below:

1. Skill based blocks are also referred to as _____.

2. Skill based blocks can be eliminated by _____

_____.

3. _____ and _____ techniques can be used

whenever a reader's purpose is to review or locate information.

4. Phrase reading refers to _____

_____.

5. Depending on the task at hand, an efficient reader will choose a reading speed at

a_____, _____, or _____ range.

Answer Key Test 1

Missing information:

1. focused on the reading material
    comprehend the information within the materials
    continue to move forward through the material

2. reading at varying speeds

3. think about the purpose for which you are reading

4. recognize self-restricting ideas and habits or blocks

5. promoting speeds that are too fast or too slow

6. psychological, physical, or skill based

7. motivation and misconceptions about reading

8. poor line tracking, over-fixating, and regression

9. physically changing body position when reading and overcoming inefficient eye movements

10. weaknesses in vocabulary and comprehension and the use of passive reading approaches

Matching:

1. d
2. c
3. e
4. b
5. a

Answer Key Test 2

Matching

1. f
2. h
3. a
4. g
5. b
6. i
7. e
8. c
9. k
10. j

Missing Information

1. method blocks

2. using active reading techniques and phrase reading

3. skimming and scanning

4. reading groups of words or more than one word at a time

5. slow, moderate, fast

Chapter Four: Vocabulary Expansion

Summary

Words are powerful tools. Many who have acquired expansive knowledge of words have used this skill to create documents that have established nations, resolved conflict between warring factions, and redefined the development of mankind.

In poetry, religious writings and, sometimes, political speeches, forceful words have stirred, uplifted and motivated people, helping them to improve their own lives and succeed in achievements that have been of great benefit to others.

Vocabulary skills are an essential part of developing highly effective reading and writing skills, but a well-developed vocabulary will also lead to an increased command of the English language that will help you improve your speaking skills. It follows suit that students who are able to speak, write, and read more efficiently are more successful in both their college and work careers, and even their personal lives.

Just as important as the vocabulary you have already acquired, the skills you use to understand new terms and the methods you employ to learn new words is extremely important in building your vocabulary. There are several strategies you can learn that will help you build your vocabulary and increase the level of comprehension, or understanding, of what you read.

To effectively develop your vocabulary, you need to identify where its needs to be expanded, what level of knowledge you have for a terms, and what learning approaches you can use to acquire new words.

Additionally, knowing word parts such as prefixes, roots, and suffixes, understanding context clues, and using dictionaries to the fullest extent are three of the best ways to understand unfamiliar terms when you come across them.

Learning word parts is a very good way to expand your vocabulary. Once you know the meaning of the various parts, you have the key to the definition of many words. Understanding context clues is another way to build your vocabulary. Context clues enable a reader to understand new words by using surrounding sentences and hints provided in the text. While context clues are helpful in grasping the meaning of unfamiliar words, you need to understand that they do not always give you a clear and precise definition of words you do not know. The most common types of context clues are definition, explanation, comparison, and contrast clues. Learning to use a dictionary can also be a valuable asset in expanding your vocabulary. A dictionary does more than just define words. Dictionaries also provide important information about such things as syllabication, pronunciation, spelling, parts of speech, and word origin.

Additionally, there are a number of memory techniques that can be used to help you learn new words including associations, graphic aids, paraphrasing, and usage. Associations help you connect the information you are trying to learn with what you already know. Graphic aids, such as clustering or brainstorming diagrams, are also helpful in remembering new information. Paraphrasing, or defining terms in your own words, is yet another way to learn new material. Finally, creating a sentence that correctly uses a term to communicate a thought is a good way to remember new terms. This process is known as usage.

Teaching Tips:

- Word games can be tremendous vocabulary building tools, so encourage students to play these kinds of games inside and outside of class. Explain how these games can reinforce study habits and make learning more enjoyable.

- Bring some publications to class that include weekly or monthly articles on how to build and improve your vocabulary.

- Suggest that students underline, circle or highlight unfamiliar words in their texts. Encourage them to make a list of the unfamiliar words and their definitions. Ask them to practice using the words in their daily conversations with others.

- When discussing reading selections in class, choose one student to take charge of the dictionary. Give that student the task of looking up any unfamiliar words that his or her classmates cannot define.

Suggested Activities:

- Have students design their own vocabulary flash cards. Suggest that visual learners used colored markers when making their cards. Have auditory learners record the words and definitions and then listen to the recording several times. Ask kinesthetic learners to use crayons when making their cards to get a waxy, smooth texture. Then have these learners run their fingers over the words.

- Have students create flash cards for common prefixes, suffixes, and roots. Use the same suggestions listed for designing vocabulary flash cards.

- Play word jeopardy using weekly vocabulary lists. First, make vocabulary cards by putting the vocabulary words and definitions on index cards. Next, divide the class into two teams and have each team select a captain. Then, take the vocabulary index cards and shuffle them thoroughly. Draw a card from the stack and call out the word to team one. Have the team confer with one another and give their answer to the team captain. Only the team captain should give the answer. Give the team a point for each correct answer. If the team gives an incorrect answer, allow team two to answer. Repeat the same process for giving team two a word as you did for team one. Play the game until you have gone through all of the vocabulary cards.

- Have students bring a newspaper article or editorial to class. Ask them to circle any unfamiliar words. Based on what they have learned about context clues, ask them to look at the way the words are used in the sentence and try to define them. After they define the words, have them use each one in a sentence.

- Select a word of the week and write it on the board. Have students define it, use it in a sentence, and practice using it in conversation inside and outside of class. Have students discuss how this practice is helping them build a broader vocabulary.

Vocabulary Expansion Test 1

Using prefix, root, and suffix meanings, choose the appropriate word to fit the sentences below.

1. Alice had been ill for a week, but once the doctor finally _____ the problem, she was able to get out of bed without feeling so nauseated.

   a. detailed
   b. diagnosed
   c. deducted

2. The bookkeeper admitted that she made a _____ when she calculated my overload pay.

   a. misfortune
   b. misconduct
   c. mistake

3. I did not pass the _____ that we were given on the first day of class.

   a. pretest
   b. preface
   c. prefix

4. I hope I will be given the chance to _____ the test.

   a. rewrite
   b. review
   c. retake

5. I am going to _____ myself in this subject because I do not want to fail the exit examination.

   a. submerse
   b. subjugate
   c. submit

6. John has sought help for his gambling addiction on many occasions, but his problem continues to _____. Recently, he was arrested for _____ money from his employer.

   a. appear; recounting
   b. resurface; embezzling
   c. precede; abducting

7. As I grew into _____, I retained many fond memories of my _____ that I have enjoyed sharing with my children.

   a. sisterhood; adulthood
   b. adulthood; childhood
   c. childhood; adulthood

8. In light of the _____ acts that occurred on September 11th, 2001,_____ has been the focus of many television programs and featured films.

   a. terrorist; heroism
   b. loyalist; capitalism
   c. communist; Nazism

9. Tara's popularity with her co-workers is a _____. Many of them have said that her lack of _____ skills is the reason that she should not seek a management position.

   a. misconception; discourse
   b. misunderstanding; dialogue
   c. misnomer; communication

10. The toddler began walking _____ his mother, but once he caught sight of the colorful flags posted at the end of the store aisles, he changed direction and headed straight for the toy department.

   a. toward
   b. afterward
   c. forward

For questions 11-15, choose the correct meaning of the underlined words in the passage below. Keep in mind that the context in which words are used can alter their meanings. Carefully review how the words are used in the sentences contained within the passage above before selecting your answers.

When you are in college, it is vital to create a personal study method that utilizes your learning style, your interests, and your creativity. The most important factor in the creation of this strategy is to be flexible; different subjects may require <u>variations</u> and parts of the method need to be modified often enough to keep your interest. There are many questions to consider such as when and where do you learn most effectively. Do you learn better when you are working with others and receiving immediate feedback, or are you an independent learner? The second most significant factor to mull over is how you will <u>formulate</u> your plan. Where will you study? Many students find it <u>advantageous</u> to study before they leave the college facility. If they run into difficulty, you may be able to find your professor and ask for help or you can go to the Learning Assistance Center where there are people to assist you. You can also leave with a clear conscience if you finish your work and review the new material you learned in class that day. It also helps to plan periodic reviews of material you have covered previously because most college classes give cumulative exams, exams on all the material covered in class during the semester. Other students may chose to work at home because of time <u>constraints</u> created by having a job, or children. Either way, plan a time, a place, and a method to study each subject you are taking.

If you are reading a text to obtain information you will need in class, some approaches can make a significant difference in the reader's ability to retain the information. The first step is to look over the chapter or assignment before you start to read; look at titles, headings, introductions, summaries, questions, and pictures. As you are doing this, work on the second step by thinking about the information you already have learned about the subjects presented in the reading. By accessing your prior knowledge about the topics from your long-term memory, you are preparing your brain to connect quickly with the new information. The last stage to use to make your study time more worthwhile is to review the information you have just learned within twelve to twenty-four hours. Research has shown that we remember the material for a much longer period if we go over the material during this time frame. The review can be involved such as using note taking practices, or it can be simply looking over the titles and subtitles in the book, asking yourself what each section covered, and answering the questions you are asking.

11. In line 3, the word variations most nearly means

    a. likenesses
    b. differences
    c. opposites
    d. types

12. In line 8, the word advantageous most nearly means

    a. helpful
    b. disadvantage
    c. disengaging
    d. inventive

13. In line 7, the word formulate most nearly means

    a. do away with
    b. hide
    c. devise
    d. wonder

14. In line 14, the word constraints most nearly means

    a. usefulness
    b. opportunities
    c. resources
    d. limits

15. In line 21, the word accessing most nearly means

    a. admitting
    b. admission
    c. contracting
    d. retrieving

Vocabulary Expansion Test 2

Choose the best word to fit the context of the sentence

1. _____ about the rise in interest rates has caused many potential investors to back away from large investment deals.

    a. Recanting
    b. Speculation
    c. Disbeliefs

2. Disease and hunger is _____ in the war torn countries of the Middle East.

    a. rampant
    b. around
    c. present

3. The meeting was such a(n) _____ one, not even those involved knew exactly what was going to be discussed until they arrived.

    a. big
    b. clandestine
    c. undercover

4. Scott is so _____ by his boss, he could barely bring himself to look at her.

    a. upset
    b. challenged
    c. intimidated

5. Matt is such a swindler, Chris was _____ into believing that the investment he made in the risky business would make him a wealthy man.

    a. talked
    b. duped
    c. convinced

5. The angry driver leaned out the window and made several _____ remarks to the woman who nearly ran him off the road.

    a. auspicious
    b. caustic
    c. departing

6. Cindy tried to provide some _____ to Joel who was very upset over the breakup with his girlfriend.

    a. happiness
    b. solace
    c. misguidance

7. Alice's _____ attitude toward her co-workers eventually caused her to lose her job.

    a. frantic
    b. belligerent
    c. mundane

8. The _____ employees threatened to walk out if their demands for improved working conditions were not met.

    a. disgruntled
    b. compatible
    c. revered

9. By her own _____, Mandy passed up a piece of chocolate cake and stuck to her diet.

    a. power
    b. admission
    c. volition

10. The noisy students became _____ once the teacher started the movie.

    a. reticent
    b. talkative
    c. stigmatized

For questions 11-15, choose the correct meaning of the underlined words in the passage below. Keep in mind that the context in which words are used can alter their meanings. Carefully review how the words are used in the sentences contained within the passage above before selecting your answers.

Toward the end of the nineteenth century, chemists noted many similarities among elements and tried to group them into certain families with <u>similar</u> properties and reactions. This was the beginning of the periodic table.

The modern periodic table places the elements according to the number and <u>arrangement</u> of the electrons in the atom. The periodic table is divided into horizontal rows and vertical columns. Each box in the table represents one element. There are over 100 known elements; thus, there are over 100 different kinds of atoms, each having its own place on the periodic table. The <u>vertical</u> columns are called groups and are labeled with Roman numerals. The <u>horizontal</u> rows are called periods and are <u>indicated</u> by Arabic numerals. (Sackheim, George I. and Lehman, Dennis D. *Chemistry for Health Sciences*. 8th ed. Upper Saddle River, NJ: Prentice Hall, 2003. p. 52).

11. In line two, the word similar most nearly means

    a. unlike
    b. alike
    c. equal
    d. not equal

12. In line four, the word arrangement most nearly means

    a. markup
    b. types
    c. layout
    d. drawing

13. In line seven, the word vertical most nearly means

    a. straight across
    b. straight up and down
    c. diagonal
    d. all around

14. In line eight, the word horizontal most nearly means

    a. straight across
    b. straight up and down
    c. diagonal
    d. all around

15. In line eight, the word indicated most nearly means

    a. hidden
    b. underlying
    c. examines
    d. shows

Answer Key Test 1

1. b
2. c
3. a
4. c
5. a
6. b
7. b
8. a
9. c
10. a
11. b
12. a
13. c
14. d
15. d

Answer Key Test 2

1. b
2. a
3. b
4. c
5. b
6. b
7. b
8. a
9. c
10. a
11. b
12. c
13. b
14. a
15. d

Chapter Five: Reading for Learning Methods

Summary

College textbooks can be challenging because they present a large amount of information in text. Technical information, multiple objectives, and visuals can make the text even more difficult. Using the study method PDQ3R (preread, divide, question, read, recite, review) can help a student address this challenging material with success.

To preread a text book, first look at the general aids provided by the author. These include the brief table of contents, the alternate table of contents, preface, glossary, answer key, appendices, and index. If CDs and websites are offered, look at the listings of information to see what information is presented and think how it relates to the other general aids in the textbook.

Look to see how the material is organized and which areas get the greatest emphasis. The Brief Table of Contents and the Preface may be the best places to find this information.

The first step to PDQ3R a chapter is to preread the chapter aids such as the title, objectives, summary, vocabulary lists, questions, and tables. Try to use the information you find in your prereading to decide the main point of the chapter. Look for the relationships between the important ideas in the chapter and think about the value of each section presented in the chapter. Use your prior knowledge to help create interest in the chapter and to create a plan for reading the chapter. Think how you can divide the information presented into smaller manageable units. Plan how you will approach the chapter and form a goal for each task you will complete. When you have completed this step, preread the section aids (bold-faced headings, bold-faced terms, graphics, inserted articles, margin notes, questions, activities, and exercises) and divide each section into suitable sections.

It is important to develop your understanding of the chapter. In order to do this, you must think about the various levels of thinking. There are six basic levels of thinking used when you read, which are somewhat sequential. They are knowledge, comprehension, application, analysis, synthesis, and evaluation. The first three levels involve lower levels of thinking and the last three use critical and independent thinking, so they are considered higher levels of thinking. The application of knowledge is the link between the two groups. It is the step in which the reader uses the information in real life situations; many students find that application can help create interest in the subject.

It is important to look at the exercises and questions presented by the author in the chapter you are reading. There are basic stems for questions for each type of thinking that you can use to decide the level of thinking the author is going to ask the reader to use. You can also create questions using these stems to elicit all the types of thinking to thoroughly understand the material in the chapter.

Marking a chapter and writing margin notes can help you to understand and remember the information more effectively. The manner in which you do these processes can use the various levels of thinking. When you consider how the material relates to other information in the chapter and analyze the information by thinking about comparisons and contrasts or advantages and disadvantages, you are using higher order thinking levels. When you judge the information and think of how it matches or differs from your opinions, you are using evaluation, the highest thinking level.

To recite and review the information, you can use many different types of methods. Answering review questions, creating flash cards, writing notes, summarizing, making maps, creating graphics, and making pictures are just a few of the methods you may want to use. Composing the information verbally or in writing can be extremely helpful. Try to use your own words, or paraphrase, because it shows understanding. Begin with the topic and use synonyms, rearrange the ideas, and combine or divide ideas to paraphrase. You should use the technical terms if accurate synonyms are not easily found. Summarizing, or writing the information in a condensed form by grouping ideas, and note taking using different formats are also very effective. Some formats for note taking are outlining (which uses a very formal specific format to show the value of each idea and the relationships between the ideas) double column notes (which list key ideas and questions in the left column and the notes in the right column), and various types of diagrams and maps (which visually show the relationships between the ideas). Using these methods will make you an effective reader.

Teaching Tips:

- Model the method for your students. It is complicated and it may take much of a class to show how you are doing each step and what you are thinking, but the students need to see and hear how it is done. Use another chapter from the book or a chapter from another textbook about a subject they need to study. One subject area to use might be a chapter on time management. Use the same chapter for the note taking assignment.

- Stress why this method is important. Tell the students that it will save them time, help them to get better grade, and improve their knowledge in a subject area. If you have a personal example of how a study method helped you or one of your students, tell them about it.

Suggested Activities:

- Provide the students with two articles about a similar subject or two versions of a fairy tale. Have the students read the articles and create a comparison contrast diagram.

- Have the students create a timeline for their life. At least 10 major events must be included on the timeline.

- Have students form groups of three. Have the students create questions for each level of thinking for one of the articles included in the text, for a group of pages from the text, or an article of your choice.

- Have pairs create a map for tone words showing the relationships between them. Use the list provided or create one of your own.

- Have the students outline five pages of the text. Have them label the titles and subtitles as suggested in the chapter, but when they go to write them on their paper have them paraphrase the headings and list the important details in their own words under the correct headings.

- Have the students use the Internet to find a description of the events at Napoleons battle at Waterloo. Have them create a timeline to use to study.

Reading for Learning Methods Test 1

1. To first understand complex textbook concepts, you must

   a. preread the material to find out how the material is organized and how the pieces relate to one another.
   b. preread the material to find the general concepts to be covered.
   c. have the right attitude and be working in a quiet place where you can concentrate.
   d. read and think of the relationships within each sentences.

2. Prereading the text and looking at the general aids in the text helps the reader to

       1. save time.
       2. understand the text.
       3. find information more quickly.
       4. comprehension insurance.

  a.   1 and 2
  b.   1 and 3
  c.   2, 3, and 4
  d.   1, 2, 3, and 4

3. The two most useful general aids for seeing how a book is organized are

   a. index and summary.
   b. brief table of contents and preface.
   c. glossary and preface.
   d. table of contents and appendices.

4. Reading the preface can usually answer which of the following questions?

   a. What are the best methods to use to read and learn the information in the text?
   b. What organization framework is used for the book and the chapters?
   c. What chapter aids will be provided?
   d. Where are the websites listed that the readers can use for reference?

5. The three types of chapter aids that should be of major focus during prereading are

   a. introductory aids, concluding aids, and the glossary.
   b. introductory aids, mid chapter aids, and concluding aids.
   c. detailed table of contents, introductory aids, and concluding aids.
   d. detailed table of contents, introductory aids, and concluding aids.

6. One of the tasks to complete as you read and think about the detailed table of contents is

   a. thinking of a mneumonic and enhancing method to remember the information for that section.
   b. forming a main idea for each section.
   c. forming a goal to match each section.
   d. look up any new words in the glossary.

7. A quick prereading of a section in a chapter will help you to avoid

   a. confusion and frustration.
   b. unnecessary rereading parts of the chapter.
   c. passive behaviors that do not help you to relate and remember information.
   d. all of the above

8. The section aid that attempts to help the reader to understand the relevance of the represented subject is the

a. graphics.
b. margin notes.
c. inserted article.
d. questions.

9. How many levels of thinking for reading and thinking purposes are relevant?

a. 6
b. 5
c. 4
d. 3

10. The three highest levels of thinking are

a. knowledge, comprehension, and application.
b. comprehension, analysis, and synthesis.
c. applications, analysis, and evaluation.
d. analysis, synthesis, and evaluation.

11. The three highest levels of thinking require the reader to go beyond the text and to use independent thinking

a. to use the information in a real life situation, to separate the information into parts, to question the information, and to mesh the information with the knowledge he or she already possesses.
b. to figure out what information was not given in the text (such as cause and effects), combine information from various sources, discuss problems with the material, and solutions not presented in the text.
c. to find stated main ideas, significant details, combine the information with information from your prior knowledge and other sources, and judge the information.
d. list trends that are indicated by the information, relate the information to real life situations, discuss problems, solutions, as well as other information for the text, and figure out causes and effects not listed in the chapter.

12. The levels of thinking can help the reader to

a. divide the author's questions into levels.
b. preread the material.
c. understand how to answer author and teacher questions, and to mark the text accordingly.
d. divide the chapter into sections.

13. Effective methods of review suggested by the author include

1. summarizing.
2. creating outlines by copying the subtitles, boldfaced print, and italicized print.
3. flashcards.
4. flow charts.

a. 1, 2, and 4
b. 1, 3, and 4
c. 1, 2, and 3

d. all of the above

14. The three methods of composing do not include

    a. making flashcards.
    b. paraphrasing.
    c. summarizing.
    d. answering review questions.

15. General aids include

    a. glossaries.
    b. headings.
    c. tables, figures, graphs.
    d. all of the above

Reading for Learning Methods Test 2

1. General and textbook aids provide the reader with

    a. the basic ideas in the text.
    b. clues about the organization of the text and signposts to find specific information.
    c. the ability to free the reader to skip sections of which the reader has prior knowledge.
    d. all of the above
    e.
2. Effective advanced marking in a text can

    1. make you actively think.
    2. improve your concentration.
    3. use annotating with basic levels of thinking.
    4. use annotating with advanced levels of thinking.

    a. 1 and 2
    b. 1, 2, and 3
    c. 1, 2, 3, and 4
    d. 1, 2, and 4

3. Note taking methods include all of the following except

    a. outlining.
    b. flash cards.
    c. maps.
    d. acronyms.

4. To take good notes you should

    a. take notes after you mark a section or finish the chapter, write the new information in your notes, make margin notes to make the ideas more understandable, use complete words to avoid the confusion that results when you use abbreviated words, and vary your methods of taking notes to match the material's organization as well as to aid understanding of the material.

    b. take notes before you mark a section or finish the chapter, take notes on the complete unit of information, add margin notes that can make your ideas clearer, use a system of abbreviations with key phrases, and use the same note taking method each time so you can do it quickly and easily.

    c. takes notes after you mark a section or finish the chapter, write the new information in your notes, make margin notes to make the ideas clearer, use complete sentences, and vary your methods of taking notes to match the material's organization as well as to aid understanding of the material.

    d. take notes after you mark a section or finish the chapter, take notes on the complete unit of information, add margin notes that can make your ideas clearer, use a shorthand system, and vary your note taking methods to help your understanding of the information and its organization.

5. Good student summaries

    a. are written in your own words.
    b. contain all the details from the chapter.
    c. are often shorter than the author's chapter summary.
    d. are written about the new ideas the student encounters in the chapter.

6. Good, flexible note takers

    a. write the new information from the reading.
    b. write the material in the same order that it is presented in the chapter.
    c. organize the information and group ideas that are related.
    d. copy the information from the chapter.

7. Outlining is one of the most frequently used effective methods for studying because an outline

    a. uses the author's words and phrases from the text, so it takes less time than summaries and taking notes.
    b. uses the author's organization, presents relationships between the point of information, and shows the level of importance of each point.
    c. uses full sentences taken from the chapter, shows the importance of the information in the manner it is arranged, and provides a note taking method that is easier to read.
    d. is easy to make as you progress through the chapter because you can use the headings to locate the new information.

8. Visuals and words in timelines and hierarchy diagrams are helpful because they reveal

    a. where the items from the paragraph are located.
    b. comparisons and contrasts.
    c. small details.
    d. relationships.

9. When you are looking at a new text, it is beneficial to look at the organization of the brief table of contents, the preface and the framework because it

    a. can help the reader find the perspective the author has on the subject.
    b. can help the reader identify the aids that are included before and after each chapter.

c. lists the chapter titles, so the reader can tell what information is covered in the book.

d. all of the above

10. Which level of thinking is used when a student makes margin notes about his/her opinions?

a. application
b. analysis
c. synthesis
d. evaluation

11. Which level of thinking is used when a reader makes a diagram listing the comparisons and contrasts about the ideas presented in the reading?

a. application
b. analysis
c. synthesis
d. evaluation

12. Which level of thinking is used when a professor asks a student to look at the textbook and related articles, and then requires the student to link the ideas between the text and the other sources?

a. application
b. analysis
c. synthesis
d. evaluation

13. Paraphrasing should

1. use technical terms and topic specific words that do not have precise synonyms.
2. use synonyms for the author's words.
3. rearrange the sentence using the author's words.
4. divide the information into smaller sentences to make it easier to understand.
5. combine points.

a. 1
b. 3
c. 1, 2, 3, and 4
d. 1, 2, 4, and 5

14. The left-hand column of double column notes is used for

a. labels, problem types, problem rules, topic words, vocabulary terms, and/ or questions.
b. information, definitions, and answers.
c. labels, problem types, information, definitions problem rules, topic words, vocabulary terms, and/ or questions.
d. notes, definitions, questions, answers, and key words.

15. Which part of the book gives background information to make some of the topics easier to understand?

    a. index
    b. preface
    c. appendices
    d. glossary

Answer Key Test 1

1. b
2. d
3. b
4. c
5. d
6. c
7. d
8. c
9. a
10. d
11. d
12. c
13. b
14. a
15. a

Answer Key Test 2

1. b
2. d
3. d
4. d
5. a
6. c
7. b
8. d
9. d
10. d
11. b
12. c
13. d
14. a
15. c

Chapter Six: Main Idea

Summary

Zeroing in on the most useful information in a paragraph or passage is an acquired skill that can only be obtained by understanding what information the author has provided and what path you must take to get through all the material. Textbooks contain an overwhelming amount of information, and while it may all be good information, all of that information is not essential to understanding the key points of what is important in the chapter. Readers can actually improve concentration and comprehension by learning to locate main ideas in paragraphs, chapters, and sections of a text and then using them to guide their reading.

Chapters in a textbook are divided into blocks that include major sections, subsections, minor sections, and paragraphs. Each block contains three structural elements: the topic—the subject of the discussion, the main idea—the author's dominant message or opinion about the topic, and the details—pieces of information that describe the topic or support the idea.

With some slight modifications, readers can use an active reading approach known as the predict and verify process to find both stated main ideas and implied main ideas in chapters and their sections. The predict and verify approach is a logical way to think about the text. This approach involves reading a small amount of information, predicting or guessing what will come next, and then reading on to verify or check your predictions.

The predict and verify approach can help improve your comprehension. Start by guessing what the topic and topic sentence are as soon as you can after you begin reading and then continuing to read to see if the details verify the predictions. Once you have verified the prediction, mark the topic, main idea, and important details in the text and record your insights in the margin of the text. Good marking is done as soon as you comprehend the text. If the materials are easy to read, you can probably mark the text as you read. If the topic is complex, you should read a little—perhaps a few sentences or a short paragraph and then go back and mark what you understand.

To find main ideas in chapters and sections of text remember that the ideas can be both broad and limited. It may take an entire chapter to cover broad ideas while it may only take a section of a chapter to cover ideas that are more limited. Ideas can also be both stated and implied. When ideas are stated, they are called the thesis; when section ideas are stated they are called the central idea. If a reader locates these ideas, along with the topics they relate to and the details they organize, it helps the construct an idea framework that simplifies the comprehension process.

Body paragraphs also contain topics, main ideas, and details. A body paragraph is a group of sentences that focus on one major point. When the ideas are stated in body paragraphs, they are referred to as the topic sentence. The topic sentence can be located in the beginning, middle, or end of a paragraph. Each of these patterns changes the order of the ideas and details and creates a shift in the reader's thinking. Each of these patterns will also change the reader's thinking in terms of using the predict and verify approach mentioned in this chapter. One thing that will help is marking the ideas so they are visually different. This technique will help you eliminate future rereading.

Teaching Tips:

- Stress to students that a good way to decide on the topic for a paragraph or passage is to first ask themselves who or what the paragraph or passage is about. Next, ask them to decide on the limiting factors that can restrict the topic. Explain that the topic must express specifically the subject (the "who" or "what") of the paragraph without having too narrow a focus. Also explain that topics must not include a broader range of subject area than is included in the writing. Tell them that topics are not complete sentences, and that they can be expressed as words or phrases.

56

- When explaining implied main idea, tell students to think of different items or people as subjects of various sentences. Help students determine how the items or people relate to each other and choose a word or phrase to group the items or people.

Use the following suggestions to help students understand and find main ideas:

Stated main ideas, or topic sentences
- include the topic, or subject, of the paragraph, and the main point the author is making about the subject.
- include some clues and keywords in the main idea that point to the organization style used in the paragraph.
- should not be too limiting; should be a broad statement that is expanded with details and support without including ideas and areas not covered in the paragraph.
- may be first sentence, but can be located anywhere in the paragraph or the passage.

To find the main idea
- look for a general sentence that includes the subject of the paragraph and the major point the author is writing about the subject.
- make sure it includes the other ideas in the paragraph.
- summarize the ideas in the paragraph and look for a sentence that states that idea.
- look for inclusive key words such as similarities, differences, events, steps, groups, categories, characteristics, meanings, examples, causes, and effects; they can also point to a main idea statement.

The remainder of the sentences
- add information that answers when, where, what, who, or why.
- give specific similarities, differences, events, steps, groups, categories, characteristics, meanings, examples, causes, and effects.

Suggested Activities:

- Supply students with passages from textbooks in other disciplines such as history, psychology, biology, and math. Have students practice Lee's predict and verify (PDQ3R) approach to locate stated main ideas and implied main ideas in these passages.

- Have students examine the titles of several longer passages. Next, ask students to concentrate on the importance of the title. Finally, ask students to write down what they think the title suggests about the topic.

- Have students look through some of the textbooks they are using in other classes and find at least three difficult sentences. Next, have the students write the sentences on three separate index cards. Then, have students work in groups of three to determine the meaning of the sentences.

- Talk to students about the elements involved in previewing. Next, examine a chapter in a textbook and ask students to pay particular attention to the heading and subheadings in the chapter. Then, based on the information gleaned from the headings and subheadings, have students jot down what they think the passage is about.

- Take stories from a newspaper and have students locate the who, what, when, where, why and how of the stories.

- Supply students with some short paragraphs, and ask them to take the paragraph apart using the five Ws model (who, what, when, where, why). Have them begin by asking who or what the passage is about. Then have them break out the details in the passage. Show them how this can help them locate the topic and main idea in the passage.

Example:

Country music and alternative music seem like very different entities, but they have a few similarities as well. The two types of music use different vocalization, volume, and rhythm styles. Alternative music has a tendency to be more discordant, strident, and pulsating, whereas country music is usually more harmonious and uses softer sounds. Country music and alternative use many of the same instruments such as the lead and bass guitars, drums, and keyboards, but country music also uses steel slide guitars. Country and alternative music both often use the lyrics of songs to tell stories and often express angst although the subjects of the sorrowful stories in country music usually deal with passionate relationships and in alternative music the anguish is related to many areas of life.

What is the passage about?
- Differences and similarities between country music and alternative music.

What are the differences between the two sounds?
- Sounds of alternative music are discordant, strident, and pulsating.
- Sounds of country music are harmonious and uses softer sounds.

What are the similarities between the two sounds?
- Country music and alternative use many of the same instruments such as the lead and bass guitars, drums, and keyboards.
- Country and alternative music both often use the lyrics of songs to tell stories and often express angst.

What is different about the stories that each type of music tells?
- Sorrowful stories in country music usually deal with passionate relationships.
- In alternative music the anguish is related to many areas of life.

Main Idea Test 1

Read the following passages and answer the questions.

Passage 1

Slow readers rarely have the experience of reading a novel or a short story at one sitting. Have you ever watched a favorite movie, one you had seen in a theater, on TV? Aren't the intensity of mood, the flow of the dialogue, the interaction of the characters, and the action of the plot rudely disturbed by all those commercials? The same can be true when a novel is read too slowly—if you always need to put it down after reading a small portion of the story. When reading more rapidly becomes automatic, you derive more pleasure from reading. (Wassman,

Rose and Rinsky, Lee Ann, Effective Reading in a Changing World, 2nd ed. Upper Saddle River, N.J: Prentice Hall, 1997. 279)

1. Which sentence best states the main idea of this passage?

    a. Slow readers rarely have the experience of reading a novel or a short story at one sitting. Have you ever watched a favorite movie, one you had seen in a theater, on TV?

    b. Aren't the intensity of mood, the flow of the dialogue, the interaction of the characters, and the action of the plot rudely disturbed by all those commercials?

    c. The same can be true when a novel is read too slowly—if you always need to put it down after reading a small portion of the story.

    d. When reading more rapidly becomes automatic, you derive more pleasure from reading.

Passage 2

"For three decades, girls (and boys, too) have been playing with and learning from Barbie, and thus she serves as an important force in conveying cultural values and attitudes. Barbie's influence is undeniable but opinions vary as to the quality of that influence on the children who play with her and on the adults they become. Barbie's critics argue that her influence has been largely detrimental, that her improbable measurements (36–18–33), her even more improbable hair, and her inexhaustible supply of clothes and accessories help perpetuate an inappropriate model of women's interests and lives. However, defenders argue that her influence has been positive, at least in part. They point out that Barbie has recently had careers such as corporate executive, airplane pilot, animal rights activist, and even presidential candidate, offering girls a chance to envision themselves being successful in the working world. Although Barbie's wedding dress is one of her most popular outfits, she's never officially married Ken (or G. I. Joe), and she remains a single, independent career woman, providing, some observers say, an alternative to the view that women's primary roles are as wives and mothers." (Petracca, M. and Sorapure, M., *Common Culture, 2nd ed.* Upper Saddle River, N.J: Prentice Hall, 1998. 8)

2. Which sentence best states the main idea of this passage?

    a. Although Barbie's wedding dress is one of her most popular outfits, she's never officially married Ken (or G. I. Joe), and she remains a single, independent career woman, providing, some observers say, an alternative to the view that women's primary roles as wives and mothers.

    b. Barbie's critics argue that her influence has been largely detrimental, that her improbable measurements (36–18–33), her even more improbable hair, and her inexhaustible supply of clothes and accessories help perpetuate an inappropriate model of women's interests and lives.

    c. Barbie's influence is undeniable but opinions vary as to the quality of that influence on the children who play with her and on the adults they become.

    d. However, defenders argue that her influence has been positive, at least in part.

Passage 3

The first four decades of the fourteenth century in Florence and Siena had been a period of political stability and economic expansion, as well as of great artistic achievement. In the 1340s, both cities suffered a series of catastrophes whose echoes were to be felt for many years. Banks and merchants went bankrupt by the score, internal upheavals shook the government, and there were repeated crop failures. Then, in 1348, the epidemic of bubonic plague—the Black Death— that spread throughout Europe wiped out more than half the population of the two cities (including, it seems, Pietro and Ambrogio Lorenzetti). Popular reactions to these events were mixed. Many people saw them as signs of divine wrath, warnings to a sinful humanity to forsake the pleasures of this earth. In such people, the Black Death aroused a mood of otherworldly exaltation. To others, such as the merry company in Boccaccios's Decameron, the fear of death intensified the desire to enjoy life while there was still time. (Janson, H. W. and Anthony, A Basic History Of Art, 6th ed. Upper Saddle River, N.J: Prentice Hall, 2002. 254)

3. The implied main idea of this paragraph is that

   a. Many people thought the people punished by the disasters in Florence and Siena during the 1340s were the sinful ones, so the survivors felt excited because divine anger had not struck them down.
   b. The disastrous events in Florence and Siena in the 1340s created in some people a yearning to enjoy life and be merry while they were alive.
   c. Many beneficial events in the early 1300s in Florence and Siena led to many positive changes in the world, but the catastrophic events during the 1340s caused people to have different types of reactions.
   d. The events in the world during the 1300s led people to have two different reactions; some people wanted to party and to enjoy life while others became more religious and conservative.

Passage 4

   Does life regularly arise from anything but life, or can it be created "spontaneously," through the coming together of basic chemical elements? The later idea had a wide acceptance from the time of the ancient Romans forward, and as late as the nineteenth century it was championed by a number of the leading scientists of the day. So how could the issue be decided? The famous French chemist and medical researcher Louis Pasteur formulated a hypothesis to address this question. He believed that many purported examples of life arising spontaneously were simple instances of airborne microscopic organisms landing on a suitable substance and then multiplying in such profusion that they could be seen. Life came from life, in other words, not from spontaneous generation. But how could this be demonstrated? In 1860, Pasteur sterilized a meat broth in glass flasks by heating it, while at the same time heating the glass necks of the flasks, after which he bent the necks into a "swan" or S-shape. The ends of the flasks remained open to the air, but inside the flasks there was not a single sign of life. Why? The broth remained sterile because microbe-bearing dust particles got trapped in the bend of the flask's neck. If Pasteur broke the neck off before the bend, however, the flask soon had a riot of bacterial life growing within it. In another test, Pasteur tilted the flask so that the broth actually touched the bend in the neck, a change that likewise got the microbes growing. (Krogh, David, Biology a Guide to the Natural World, 2nd ed. Upper Saddle River, N.J: Prentice Hall, 2002. 8)

4. The implied main idea of this paragraph is that

   a. In the past, some people believed life could be created spontaneously by combining different elements.
   b. As late as the nineteenth century people were still arguing about how life could be created; some thought it could only come from life and others felt it could be made from combining various elements.
   c. In 1860, Louis Pasteur completed an experiment to demonstrate that life came from life.
   d. In 1860, Louis Pasteur conducted research experiments to illustrate the life could be created spontaneously.

Passage 5

In 2000, more than half the U.S. population over age 15 were Internet users. Yet these users are not average people; they represent an information elite, privileged in more ways than one. About 95 percent are white (compared to 85 percent of the population), 60 percent are men (compared to half the population), and 40 percent are professionals, or managers (compared to 18 percent of the population. In short, computer users are people with above-average incomes. College students stand out among computer users, but even among them, differences emerge. Students attending private (and more expensive) colleges and universities are likely to be more frequent e-mail users than those attending public institutions. Similarly, students at two-year and at historically black colleges also make less use of computers. The unequal spread of computer skills indicates that a link between new information technology and social inequality exists. (Adapted from Macionis, John J. Sociology, 9th ed. Upper Saddle River, NJ: Prentice Hall, 2003. 406)

5. Which sentence best states the main idea of this passage?

   a. College students that attend four-year colleges are more technologically advanced than two-year college students and students who attend traditionally black colleges.
   b. The unequal spread of computer skills indicates that a link between new information technology and social inequality exists.
   c. More young adults are using the Internet and new technology than older people.
   d. Around the world, computer use is growing rapidly, especially among the young.

Passage 6

The average student spends a lot of time thinking about his or her body and ways to make it more attractive. While most people realize that there are a wide range of body types and sizes, attractiveness tends to be more narrowly defined by the images of men and women we see in the popular media; and nearly all media images equate attractiveness and desirability with a limited range of body types.

For men, the image of a tall, broad-shouldered, muscular man with so little body fat that every muscle is visible is portrayed as most desirable.

The standards for female beauty are unforgiving also. Images of female beauty are almost exclusively women with small hips; long, thin limbs; large breasts; and no body fat.

This is virtually the only image of female beauty seen in fashion magazines, on billboards, on television, and in the movies.

Into this milieu steps the average college students—worried about appearance, trying to find time to study, exercise, and socialize and now making all his or her own decisions about food, often on a limited budget.

Making choices that are good for long-term health is not easy. The typical dining-center meal-plan choices, often greasy and fat-laden, are available in unlimited portions. The difficulty of making healthful choices is compounded by the presence of campus snack shops, vending machines, and conveniently located fast-food restaurants that offer time-pressed students easily accessible, inexpensive foods containing little nutrition. Coupling tremendous pressure to be thin with a glut of readily available unhealthful foods can lead to the establishment of unhealthful eating habits that persist far beyond college life. In many cases, these conflicting pressures can lead students to develop eating habits that result in a lifelong battle with obesity or starvation, along with their associated health risks. (Material in this passage was adapted from Belk, Colleen and Virginia Borden. *Biology Science for Life. 1ʳ ed.* Upper Saddle River, NJ: Prentice Hall, 2004. 23)

6. The implied main idea for paragraph one is that

   a. The media's idea of beauty and allure encompasses few body types and few different viewpoints.
   b. The media equates attractiveness and desirability with being a beautiful college student.
   c. College students spend a lot of time thinking about making their bodies look attractive as it is portrayed in the media.
   d. Many people realize that beauty can encompass a wide variety of body shapes and types, which is unlike the media viewpoints of beauty.

Passage 7

Yelling or shouting at children, spanking, and other forms of corporal punishment are not an effective manner in which to communicate or control inappropriate behavior so they should not be used. Instead of controlling inappropriate behavior, these behaviors simply provide children with inappropriate models of behavior. When a caregiver resorts to the use of corporal punishment, chances are that the caregiver is out of control. In this case, the caregiver should be given a break and, if possible, let someone else take over for a while. These kinds of caregiver behaviors are not only ineffective in changing the behavior of children, but also damaging to children's self-esteem. In the end, nothing worthwhile has been accomplished, and the potential for negative outcomes is great. (Zirpoli, Thomas J. and Mellov, Kristine J., Behavior Management. Upper Saddle River, N.J: Prentice Hall, 2001. 305)

7. Which sentence best states the main idea of this passage?

   a. Caregivers who are out of control should not be allowed to stay with the children who are usually under their care.
   b. Yelling or shouting at children, spanking, and other forms of corporal punishment are not an effective manner in which to communicate or control inappropriate behavior so they should not be used.
   c. There is never an appropriate time to use corporal punishment with children because it provides the children with a bad role model.
   d. Aggressive behavior by caregivers is an effective way of disciplining children when they are out of control.

Passage 8

Back when students had to do their writing on a typewriter, the preparation of a document was so time consuming that having a draft that was close to perfection was essential before the student even started to type. Then the emphasis was on correct typing that made the revision process difficult at best. Now that we have access to word processing, the best thing you can do is to not start out worrying about perfection. Allow the creative right side of your brain to let your thoughts flow. Revising and editing will be easier when you use the technology available to you, so write with abandon when you start. Don't worry about spelling and commas. Later, you can cut and paste and use spelling and grammar checkers to polish you writing before you submit your assignment to your instructor. Concentrate on expressing your ideas when you start. The rest can all be fixed later. (Thiroux, Emily, The Critical Edge Thinking and Researching in a Virtual Society, Upper Saddle River, N.J: Prentice Hall, 1999. 53)

8. The implied main idea of this paragraph is that

    a. When students had to use typewriters to type their papers, it was important to make your first draft on the typewriter almost perfect because it took so long to retype it.
    b. Computers with cut and paste options and spelling and grammar checkers are now so advanced that it is not necessary to take the time to make your first draft close to perfect; it is okay just to type using the creative right side of your brain to let the ideas flow and then revise it later.
    c. Typing a paper is much easier now than it was in the past.
    d. In times past when typewriters were used to type drafts for documents, it was important to take a lot of time to create an almost perfect draft, but in the present you can use technology to help you create your draft, so you can first let the ideas flow as you type and later go back to revise it.

Passage 9

Cancer is not one disease but many. Some forms are particularly susceptible to radiation therapy. The aim of radiation therapy is to destroy cancerous cells before too much damage is done to healthy tissue. Radiation is most lethal to rapidly producing cells, and this is precisely the characteristic of cancer cells that allows radiation therapy to be successful. Radiation is carefully aimed at cancerous tissue while minimizing the exposure of normal cells. If the cancer cells are killed by the destructive effects of the radiation, the malignancy is halted. Patients undergoing radiation therapy often get sick from the treatments. Nausea and vomiting are the usual early symptoms of radiation sickness. Radiation therapy can also interfere with white blood cell replenishment and increase susceptibility to infection. (Hill, John W. and Kolb, Doris K., Chemistry for Changing Times, 10th ed. Upper Saddle River, N.J: Prentice Hall, 2004.100)

9. The implied main idea of the first paragraph is that

    a. Cancer is many different diseases that can be treated by various types of treatment.
    b. Radiation can damage cells and prevent them from creating new cells.
    c. Cancer is a group of different diseases that share common characteristics.
    d. Radiation therapy may stop certain types of cancers.

Passage 10

Your stomach expands when you've just had a big meal, but then contracts when you've been busy for a few hours. Your heart expands and contracts probably 70 times a minute. You bend over to tie your shoes and, unbeknownst to you, many of your internal organs slide out of the way. What allows you to do all this? The answer is an internal space you have: a large, fluid filled body cavity. We humans are not alone in having such a cavity, or coelom. Very few animal groups do not have this cavity.

What's the value of such a cavity? Well, first, an expandable stomach has the same value as a gas tank: It allows you to go awhile without refueling. Then there is the fact that if a heart couldn't expand and contract, it wouldn't work at all. Thirdly, a body cavity provides organs with protection from bodily blows and provides a large part of the body with flexibility.

In most instances, the coelom surrounds another physical structure, the digestive tract—meaning the tube, functioning in the digestion, that runs from the mouth to the anus. We can therefore think of the coelom as one tube that encircles another; the coelom is generally tube-shaped, and it surrounds the tube that is the digestive tract. (There are, however, lots of variations on this general principle.)

The concept of a coelom is intimately linked to that of tissue layers. All animal embryos have what are known as germ layers, meaning layers of cells that become various types of tissue in adult animals. Most animals have three types of germ layers: endoderm an inside layer, mesoderm a middle layer; and ectoderm an outer layer. The linkage between the coelom and the mesoderm provides a way of formally defining the coelom which is the central body cavity in an animal that is lined with cells of mesodermal origin. (Adapted from Krogh, David, Biology a Guide to the Natural World, 2nd ed. Upper Saddle River, N.J: Prentice Hall, 2002. 440–441)

10. Which statement best states the main idea of the passage?

    a. A large, fluid filled body cavity called the coelom allows our heart to expand and contract as it beats.

    b. A large, fluid filled body cavity called the coelom allows our digestive system to work properly, so we can process the food we eat.

    c. A large, fluid filled body cavity called the coelom allows our bodies to work correctly, gives us flexibility, and protects us from injuries and blows.

    d. A large, fluid filled body cavity called the coelom allows our bodies to be protected from blows from other people and other objects.

Match the following terms to the correct definition:

_____1. details	a. a group of sentences that focus on one major point
_____2. predict and verify	b. author's dominant message or opinion about a topic
_____3. body paragraphs	c. pieces of information that describes the topic or supports the idea
_____4. textbook blocks	d. a process that can be used to find both stated main ideas and implied main ideas in chapters and their sections
_____5. main idea	e. includes major sections, subsections, minor sections, and paragraphs

Main Idea Test 2

Read the following passages and answer the questions.

Passage 1

    As an interesting exercise, carry a trash bag around for a single day and collect everything you throw away. Most people are surprised to find that the average person in the United States discards almost 5 pounds of paper, metal, plastic, and other materials daily (over a lifetime, that's about 50 tons). For the country as a whole, this amounts to about 1 billion pounds of solid waste each and every day.

    As a rich nation containing people who value convenience, the United States has become a disposable society. We consume more products than virtually any other nation on Earth, and much of them have throwaway packaging. The most familiar case is fast food, served with cardboard, plastic, and styrofoam containers that we throw away within minutes. However, countless other products—from film to fishhooks—are elaborately packaged to make the product more attractive to the customer and discourage tampering and theft.

Consider, too, that manufacturers market soft drinks, beer, and fruit juices in aluminum cans, glass, jars, and plastic containers, which not only consume finite resources but also generate mountains of solid waste. Then there are countless items intentionally designed to be disposable: pens, razors, flashlights, batteries, even cameras. Other goods, from light bulbs to automobiles, are designed to have limited useful life and then become unwanted junk. As Paul H. Connett, author of "The Disposable Society," points out, even the words we use to describe what we throw away "waste," "litter," "trash," "refuse," "garbage," rubbish"—show how little we value what we cannot immediately use.

Living in a rich society, the average person in the United States consumes 50 times more steel, 170 times more newspaper, 250 times more gasoline, and 300 times more plastic each year than the typical person in India. This high level of consumption means that we in the United States not only use a disproportionate share of the planet's natural resources but also generate most of the world's refuse.

We like to say that we "throw things away." But 80 percent of our solid waste is not burned or recycled and never "goes away." Rather, it ends up in landfills, which are, literally, filling up. Materials in landfills also can pollute groundwater. Although in most places laws now regulate what can be discarded in a landfill, the Environmental Protection agency has identified 30,000 dump sites across the United States containing hazardous materials that are polluting water both above and below the ground. In addition, what goes into landfills all too often stays there, sometimes for centuries. Tens of millions of tires, diapers, and other items that we bury in landfills each year do not decompose and will be an unwelcome legacy for future generations.

Environmentalists argue that we should address the problem of solid waste by doing what many of our ancestors did: Turn "waste" into a resource. One way to do this is through recycling, reusing resources we would otherwise discard. Recycling is an accepted practice in Japan and many other nations, and it is becoming more common in the United States, where we now reuse about 30 percent of waste materials. The share is increasing as laws mandate reuse of certain materials such as glass bottles and aluminum cans. In addition, because our nation has a market-based economy, recycling is bound to increase as it becomes more profitable. (Marconis, John J., Society The Basics. 7th ed. Upper Saddle River, NJ: Prentice Hall, 2004. 424–425)

1. Which statement best states the main idea for the passage?

   a. The United States produces much of the world's refuse and uses many of the world's natural resources because we are a rich nation and we are materialistic.
   b. Recycling is good for the earth because it reuses many of our natural resources and thus saves some of the resources for others in other countries on this earth.
   c. The Unites States uses more natural resources and creates more trash than other countries, so our nation should take measures to save our resources and make less trash.
   d. The nations of the world should embrace the concept of recycling in order to save natural resources and to create less trash.

Passage 2

The Neolithic Revolution placed us on a level at which we might well have remained indefinitely. The forces of nature would never again challenge men and women as they had Paleolithic peoples. In a few places, however, the balance between humans and nature was upset by a new threat, one posed not by nature but by people themselves. Evidence of that threat can be seen in the earliest Neolithic fortifications, built almost 9,000 years ago in the Near East. What was the source of the human conflict that made these defenses necessary? Was it competition for grazing land among herders or for arable soil among farming communities? The basic cause, we suspect, was that the Neolithic Revolution had been too successful. It had allowed population groups to grow beyond the available food supply. This situation might have been resolved in a number of ways. Constant warfare could have reduced the population. Or the people could have united in larger and more disciplined social units for the sake of group efforts—such as building fortifications—that no loosely organized society could achieve on its own.

We do not know the outcome of the struggle in the region, but excavations may tell us how far the urbanizing process extended. But about 3,000 years later, similar conflicts, on a larger scale, arose in the Nile Valley and again in the plains of the Tigris and Euphrates rivers. The pressures that forced the people in these regions to abandon Neolithic village life may well have been the same. These conflicts created enough pressure to produce the first civilization. To be civilized, after all, means to live as a citizen, a town dweller. (The word civilization derives from the Latin term for city, civilis.) These new societies were organized into much larger units—cities and city-states—that were far more complex and efficient than had ever existed before. First in Mesopotamia and Egypt, somewhat later in neighboring areas, and in the Indus Valley and along the Yellow river in China, people would henceforth live in a more dynamic world. Their ability to survive was challenged not by the force of nature but by human forces, by tensions and dissent arising either within society or as the result of competition between societies. Efforts to cope with such forces have proven to be a far greater challenge than the earlier struggle with nature. The problems and pressures faced by historic societies thus are very different from those faced by people in the Paleolithic and Neolithic eras.

These momentous changes also spurred the development of new technologies in what we term the Bronze Age and the Iron Age, which, like the Neolithic, are stages, not distinct eras. People first began to cast bronze, an alloy of copper and tin, in the Middle East around 3500 B.C., at the same time that the earliest cities arose in Egypt and Mesopotamia. The smelting and forging of iron were invented about 2000-1500 B.C. by the Hittites, an Indo-European-speaking people who settled in Cappadocia (today's east central Turkey), a high plateau with abundant copper for mineral resources that helped create the conflicts that beset civilizations everywhere. (Adapted from Janson, H. W. and Anthony, A Basic History Of Art, 6th ed. Upper Saddle River, N.J: Prentice Hall. 2002. 254)

2. Which statement best states the main idea for the passage?

   a. Pressures in society that started in Neolithic times caused the people to build fortifications and to engage in conflicts.
   b. Pressures in society that started as a result of the Neolithic Revolution changed the manner in which people lived and spurred the people to create new civilizations and inventions.
   c. In Mesopotamia and Egypt, somewhat later in neighboring areas, and in the Indus Valley and along the Yellow river in China, people created civilized towns and cities.
   d. New technologies were created because of the cities that had been created in Mesopotamia and Egypt, somewhat later in neighboring areas, and in the Indus Valley and along the Yellow River in China.

Passage 3

Darwin was born on February 12, 1809, in the country town of Shrewsbury, England. He was the son of a prosperous physician, Robert Darwin, and his wife, Susannah Wedgewood Darwin, who died when Charles was eight. Young Charles seemed destined to follow in his father's footsteps as a doctor, being sent away to the University of Edinburgh at age sixteen for medical training. But he found medical school boring, and his medical career came to a halt when, in the days before anesthesia, he found it unbearable to watch surgery being performed on children. His father then decided that he should study for the ministry. At the age of twenty, Darwin set off for Cambridge University to spend three years that he later recalled as "the most joyous in my happy life." Darwin's happiness came in part from the fact that theology at Cambridge took a backseat to what had been his true passion since childhood: the study of nature. From his early years, he had collected rock, animal, and plant specimens and was an avid reader of nature books. His studies at Cambridge did yield a divinity degree, but they also gave Darwin a solid background in what we would today call life science and Earth science.

Darwin's training, and the contacts he made at school, came together in one of the most fateful first-job offers ever extended to a recent college graduate. One of Darwin's Cambridge professors arranged to have him be the resident naturalist aboard the HMS Beagle. This was a ship that was to undertake a survey of coastal areas around the world. In addition to numerous stops on the east coast of South America (the ship's primary survey site), the Beagle also stopped briefly at the remote Galapagos Islands, about nine hundred seventy kilometers or six hundred miles west of Ecuador.

Thus did Darwin spend time on a research vessel—five years in all—beginning in England two days after Christmas 1831 and ending back there in October 1836. Just twenty-two when he left, he was prone to seasickness; he had to share a 10-by-15-foot room with two other officers; he was not a traveler by nature; and the journey was dangerous. Three of the Beagle's officers died because of illness during it. Yet Darwin was happy because of the work he was doing: looking, listening, collecting, and thinking about it all. (Adapted from Krogh, David, Biology a Guide to the Natural World, 2nd ed. Upper Saddle River, N.J: Prentice Hall, 2002. 324–325)

3. The implied main idea of the first paragraph is that

   a. Darwin spent much of his life in nineteenth-century England doing whatever his father wished for him to do.
   b. Darwin's early life and education in nineteenth-century Britain led him to develop an interest in life and Earth sciences.
   c. Darwin spent much of his life in nineteenth-century England getting university degrees at Cambridge and the University of Edinburgh.
   d. Darwin's early life and education in nineteenth-century Britain led him to develop an interest in medicine, but he could not manage seeing children have surgery.

Passage 4

Friction refers to the ever-present resistance to motion that occurs whenever two materials, or media, are in contact with each other. This resistance occurs for all types of media—solids, liquids, and gases—and is characterized as the force of friction.

In some situations, we want to increase friction, for example by putting sand on an icy road or sidewalk to improve traction. This might seem contradictory, since an increase in friction presumably would increase the resistance to motion. However, consider the forces involved in walking. Without friction, the foot would slip backwards. (Think about walking on a slippery surface.) The force of friction prevents this, and sometimes needs to be increased on slippery surfaces. In other situations, we try to reduce friction. For instance we lubricate moving machine parts to allow them to move more freely, lessen wear, and reduce expenditure of energy. Automobiles would not run without friction-reducing oils and greases.

All surfaces are microscopically rough, no matter how smooth they appear or feel. It was originally thought that friction was primarily due to the mechanical interlocking of surface irregularities, or asperities (high spots). However, research has shown that the friction between the contacting surfaces of ordinary solids (metals in particular) is mostly due to local adhesion. When surfaces are pressed together, local welding or bonding occurs in a few small patches where the largest asperities make contact. To overcome this local adhesion, a force great enough to pull apart the bonded regions must be used. Once contacting surfaces are in relative motion, another form of friction may result when the asperities of a harder material dig into a softer material, with a "plowing "effect.

Friction between solids is generally classified into three main types: static, sliding (kinetic), and rolling. Static friction includes all cases in which the frictional force is sufficient to prevent relative motion between surfaces. Sliding friction, or kinetic friction, occurs when there is relative (sliding) motion at the interface of the surfaces in contact. Rolling friction, such as occurs between a train wheel and a rail, is attributed to local deformations in the contact region. This type of friction is somewhat difficult to analyze. (Adapted from Wilson, Jerry D., College Physics, 2nd ed. Upper Saddle River, N.J. Prentice Hall, 1994. 123–124)

4. Which statement best states the main idea, or central point, for the passage?

   a. Friction, the ever-present resistance to motion that occurs whenever two materials, or media, are in contact with each other, is caused by local adhesion.
   b. Friction, the ever-present resistance to motion that occurs whenever two materials, or media, are in contact with each other, is caused by the roughness of a harder material as it digs into a softer material.
   c. Friction, the ever-present resistance to motion that occurs whenever two medias are in contact with each other, can be divided into three categories.
   d. Friction, the ever-present resistance to motion that occurs whenever two materials, or media, make contact with each other, has two basic causes and can be divided into three main types.

Passage 5

Prehistoric humans spent only 40 percent of their waking hours on the necessities of life, such as food and shelter, according to anthropologists. That left 60 percent for "leisure" pursuits—napping, grooming, story telling, painting pictograms on cave walls, and dreaming up the wheel, the knife, and who knows, maybe the Veg-O-Matic. Despite the proliferation of "labor-saving" devices ranging from microwave ovens to drip-irrigations systems, modern humans seem to have less time than their long-lost ancestors. Visions of a twenty-hour work week, a noble idea proposed by Bertrand Russell in the 1930s, have never come to pass. In fact, as the global and domestic economy sags, many people find themselves working fifty and sixty hours a week just to get by. In this culture, our sense of identity and even self-worth is measured largely by the work that we do, rather than by what we do with our spare time. In fact, the very subjective "spare" suggests that any time left over from work is of lesser importance. Paradoxically, however, what we do in our spare time more often defines our personalities than what we do from nine to five. Certainly for some people, their professional career is congruent with personal satisfaction, but for many, work is the way to pay the bills, while leisure is an opportunity to pursue activities that truly nurture them. Juliet Schor, in her essay "Exiting the Squirrel Cage," takes this argument a step further drawing a distinction between "unpaid work" and "true leisure" time. Yet ironically, it is this tiny fraction of "true leisure" time that plays what some would argue the most important role in defining us as unique individuals. As Witold Rybczynski suggests, our attitudes toward leisure and our leisure pursuits also serve to define us as a culture. (Petracca, M. and Sorapure, M. Common Culture, 2nd ed. Upper Saddle River, N.J: Prentice Hall, 1998. 528–529)

5. What is the central point of this paragraph?

   a. Prehistoric humans spent more of their lives pursuing leisure activities than on taking care of the necessities of life such as seeking food and finding shelter, whereas people of today work many hours because we view ourselves by our work.
   b. Even though our society has more laborsaving devices, we spent much of our time working more than forty-hour weeks.
   c. Unlike cave dwellers, in the present time people in this culture spend much of their time working because we view our identity and self worth by the work we do.
   d. Today, unlike in the past, people in this culture spend much of their time working because we view our individuality and self-esteem by the work we do, but really our leisure time activities define us as distinctive individuals.

To answer questions 6-20, read the passage below and complete the cluster diagram outlining the main idea, major details, and minor details in the paragraph.

Most people have a preferred style of learning that enables them to learn more quickly and effectively. Some people are visual learners; they gather knowledge by seeing the information. They learn the best by visually examining texts, items, pictures, or videos. An anatomy professor at one campus offers students an opportunity to buy a coloring book of the human body because his visual learners find that coloring different systems of the body specific colors helps them to remember the relationships between the body parts. Another learning style would be auditory learning, which would include the people who learn most effectively by listening. Lectures, tapes, songs, and CDs would help the auditory learner. A third learning style is kinesthetic or tactile learning. The people in this group gain knowledge by moving, doing, and touching. Typing, writing, and activities requiring movements would be good activities for learners in this category. One of my students who learned kinesthetically made up cheers that used her vocabulary words and their meanings, and as a result she received extremely high grades in vocabulary.

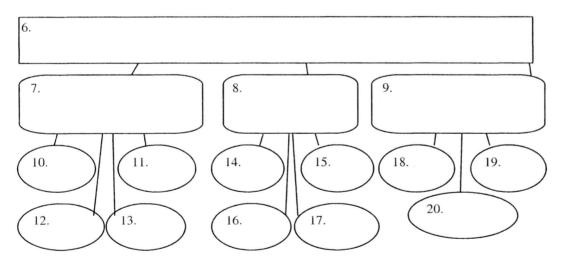

69

Answer Key Test 1

1. D
2. C
3. D
4. C
5. B
6. C
7. B
8. D
9. D
10. C

Matching

1. C
2. D
3. A
4. E
5. B

Answer Key Test 2

1. C
2. B
3. D
4. D
5. D

Cluster Diagram

Main Idea

6. Learning styles are a preferred style of learning that enables learners to learn more quickly and effectively.

Major Details

7. Visual learners learn by seeing the information.

8. Auditory learners learn by hearing.

9. Kinesthetic learners learn by touching, doing, and moving.

Minor Details for Visual Learners:

10. Use videos

11. Use books

12. Use pictures

13. Use items

Minor Detail for Auditory Learners:

14. Use CDs

15. Use songs

16. Use tapes

17. Use lectures

Minor Details for Kinesthetic Learners:

18. Use typing

19. Use writing

20. Use body actions

Chapter Seven: Details and Logical Patterns

Summary

Textbook chapters use extensive details to give students information about the subject and effectively support the presented ideas. Efficient readers scrutinize the multifaceted text information and think about the relationships between the ideas and the types of information.

Informational texts make use of facts, examples, descriptions, definitions, and references as details. Facts are provable ideas, descriptions depict a sensory or emotional portrayal of the information, definitions give meanings, examples give specific illustrations of the ideas, and references present ideas from other sources. Major details support the main ideas of the paragraphs in the selection; they prove and clarify the main ideas. They often address the answers to the what, how, or why questions you have created about the main ideas. Details that support and develop the major details, instead of the main ideas, are minor details. They present examples of a major detail or they provide the answers to the questions that start with the words when, who, and why.

It is important to see how the details relate to one another in order to divide the major and minor details. You can mark the details in the text and label the major and minor details with specific markings. You can also number the details. Both methods will make them stand out from the main ideas when you review the material. The predict and verify process will enable you to divide the major details from the minor details more easily.

The author presents the ideas in the text chapters in logical patterns or relationships by the way the information is related. Identifying the logical pattern of the material helps the reader to predict the ideas in the reading, decide how the ideas relate to one another, understand the ideas, and remember the information more easily. Six common patterns are: list in which the items of equal value are given in no specific order, definition in which meanings are given, sequence in which events or steps are given in chronological order, classification in which a large group is divided into smaller groups by using specific characteristics, comparison/contrast in which likenesses and difference between the subjects are stressed, and cause/effect in which reasons and consequences are given. The sequence pattern can be further divided into chronological order that lists events in chronological order, and process that lists steps or stages in sequential order. Additional logical patterns include statement and clarification in which an idea and an explanation are given, spatial order in which the placement of the objects is emphasized, order of importance in which the value of each idea or object is accentuated, and summary in which the ideas are given in a concise manner. These patterns are found within sentences, paragraphs, or readings of multiple paragraphs. Specific words called signal words can assist the reader to identify the logical pattern the author is using. The signal words are usually located in the topic sentence or main idea.

The patterns guide the reader when they are creating order in the ideas presented by the author. you can use the patterns to make maps, outlines, notes, flow charts, and other study aids.

Teaching Tips:

- Introduce the patterns by presenting the students with sentences for each pattern. Map each of the sentences. The visual examples help the students to see the relationships more easily.

- Have individual students state a sentence for each pattern. This can help the students by having them hear a sentence that they might relate to more easily. If you can have them come up with humorous statements, it does make it more fun.

Suggested Activities:

- Form teams of three people. Have each team look through their textbooks to find a paragraph on which to work. Have them write the topic on an index card or an overhead plastic sheet, the main idea on a separate index card or an overhead plastic sheet, and each detail on a separate index card or an overhead plastic sheet. Number each card or overhead plastic sheet with a different number. Present each card under an Elmo or the plastic sheets on an overhead. Present each sheet for 20 seconds. Have the students write the number of the card or sheet and then have the teams have to write whether the presented slide is a main idea, detail, or topic. Go over the answers as a group.

- Have the students think back to their first day of college. Have them create a main idea about that day. An example might be, "The first day of college was overwhelming." Then the students must create five major details for support of the main idea and ten minor ideas to support the major ideas.

- Have each student bring in a picture where something is happening. Have them write ten major details about the picture and ten minor details about the picture.

- Form groups of two or three. Have each group create a top ten list of situations in which recognizing the relationship of the reading can help the reader.

- Give each group a list of the relationship patterns. Have each group write an example sentence for each pattern. Have each group hand in their papers. Hand them out to different groups and have the groups write the pattern for each sentence. You could process these as a large group by having the students read the sentence and state which pattern they chose, putting the sentence sheets under an Elmo and discussing the second groups pattern label, or you can collect them and correct them.

Details and Logical Patterns Test 1

Read the passages and answer the questions.

Passage One

DNA fingerprinting can be used to establish parentage, convict a criminal, exonerate the innocent, and identify the dead. Courts around the world have allowed DNA fingerprinting to be used as evidence in hundreds of murder and rape cases. Many people have been released from prison on the basis of DNA that was present on items that were admitted into evidence and saved in case of an appeal. The United States Army collects DNA samples from all enlisted personnel to facilitate identification of those who are killed during war. Even private citizens can purchase kits that help establish parentage; cells scraped from inside the cheek of purported parents and children can be sent away for accurate and inexpensive DNA analysis by private companies,

The real power of this technique is that it can provide positive identification with great accuracy. More conventional methodologies, such as blood typing, can only exclude people who do not match the blood type of the person in question, and are not as useful to confirm a positive identification. (Belk, Colleen and Borden, Virginia, Biology Science for Life, 1st ed. Upper Saddle River, N.J. Prentice Hall, 2004. 139)

1. The first paragraph is organized by

   a. listing order.
   b. cause and effect order.
   c. comparison and contrast order.
   d. sequential order.

2. According to the passage, DNA samples are taken from all

   a. children, so parentage can be determined.
   b. criminals to determine who raped a person.
   c. enlisted personnel to facilitate identification of those who are killed during a war.
   d. enlisted Army personnel to facilitate identification of victims of wars.

3. What types of details are in the first paragraph?

   a. facts
   b. examples
   c. descriptions
   d. definitions

Passage Two

   Consider this question: "Why does Eveline stay with her abusive father?" As you think, start writing. Set down everything that comes to mind. Write in complete sentences, but do not concern yourself with spelling, word choice, or punctuation. You are writing for your own benefit, attempting to discover everything about Eveline's decision that you have in mind after reading and thinking about the story.
   After writing for ten minutes (or after you run out of ideas), stop and read over what you have said. Underline any ideas that might serve as the focus for the paper. Put stars or asterisks in the margin beside any ideas that sound useful for your interpretation. (McMahan, Elizabeth, Day, Susan, and Funk, Robert., Literature and the Writing Process, 6th ed. Upper Saddle River, N.J: Prentice Hall, 2002. 11)

4. For this passage, the author uses an overall organizational pattern of

   a. simple listing order.
   b. comparison and contrast order.
   c. cause/effect order.
   d. sequential/process order.

5. According to this passage,

   a. you should outline and plan your paper before you start to write.
   b. you should first write your ideas as they come to mind.
   c. you should first answer the question by brainstorming ideas; write key words and ideas on your paper.
   d. you should use proper grammar and punctuation when you start to write your answer to the question.

Passage Three

Three teachers in my life shaped my future. Mrs. Rhine, my sixth grade teacher, taught me to believe in my abilities and to be happy using them. A new world opened up to me because of Mrs. Rhine's encouragement and her stimulating creative, student assignments. Although I had only been an average student in the earlier grades, throughout the sixth grade, my grades improved steadily, and I earned the right to be in the honors section in junior high school. The second teacher that affected my life was Mr. Ponte because he taught me to question what people stated and to observe the world with a questioning eye. Up to this point in my life, I had accepted ideas I read in the newspaper and in books, but he taught me to weigh the evidence and the support that was presented in order to make my own decisions. The third teacher that had an effect on me was Dr. Schillit because he taught me to set goals, to see the wonders of the world, and to challenge myself to go further. He continuously challenged me to try new ideas and to think of the possibilities for my life. Without the influence of these three teachers, I would not be the person I am today. (Levine-Brown, Patti, Hughes, Suzanne, and Ciez-Volz, Kathleen, The Prentice Hall Florida Exit Test Study Guide for Writing, Upper Saddle River, N.J: Prentice Hall, 2004. 24.)

6. Which type of logical pattern is used in this paragraph?

   a. cause and effect
   b. classification
   c. comparison and contrast
   d. definition

7. According to the passage, Mr. Ponte strongly affected this person's life because

   a. was encouraging and stimulating.
   b. taught the writer to be happy using the writer's abilities.
   c. taught the writer to question what people stated and wrote.
   d. challenged the writer and taught the writer to set goals.

Passage Four

Many people feel that reading quickly will make understanding more difficult, but if you are taught the proper methods, reading efficiently usually leads to better comprehension. Many efficient readers learn to like reading. Good readers prepare to read by using one of the previewing methods before they settle down to their serious reading. The first is to scan the whole chapter to get an understanding of the topic and the aspects covered in the reading, and the second is to survey specific parts of the chapter or article to find out information about topics covered in the reading. After completing either of these previews, you should take a minute to think about your prior knowledge of the subject in order to pull the knowledge from your memory. Amazingly, just using one of these two methods usually doubles a person's reading speed and increases his or her understanding. The third step to reading capably and quickly is to practice reading proficiently by timing your reading and setting goals to make you read just a little bit faster each time. Finally, after each period of reading, check your comprehension by telling someone about the material you have read or by writing notes about the reading. (Levine-Brown, Patti, Hughes, Suzanne, and Ciez-Volz, Kathleen, The Prentice Hall Florida Exit Test Study Guide for Writing, Upper Saddle River, N.J: Prentice Hall, 2004. 26)

8. Which type of logical thinking pattern is used in this paragraph?

   a. listing order
   b. classification order
   c. comparison and contrast order
   d. sequential/process order

9. What logical thinking pattern signal words are used in this paragraph?

   a. difficult, usually, many
   b. quickly, completing, reading
   c. amazingly, capably, faster
   d. after, third, finally

10. According to the passage, good readers

   a. scan the chapter or survey specific parts of the chapter before they settle down to read.
   b. open their book to the correct page and read very quickly with good comprehension.
   c. read other articles or chapters to find out information about topics covered in the reading.
   d. write notes about the topics covered in the chapter or article as they read.

Passage Five

Darwin was born on February 12, 1809, in the country town of Shrewsbury, England. He was the son of a prosperous physician, Robert Darwin, and his wife, Susannah Wedgewood Darwin, who died when Charles was eight. Young Charles seemed destined to follow in his father's footsteps as a doctor, being sent away to the University of Edinburgh at age sixteen for medical training. But, he found medical school boring and his medical career came to a halt when, in the days before anesthesia, he found it unbearable to watch surgery being performed on children. His father then decided that he should study for the ministry. At the age of twenty, Darwin set off for Cambridge University to spend three years that he later recalled as "the most joyous in my happy life." Darwin's happiness came in part from the fact that theology at Cambridge took a backseat to what had been his true passion since childhood: the study of nature. From his early years, he had collected rock, animal, and plant specimens and was an avid reader of nature books. His studies at Cambridge did yield a divinity degree, but they also gave Darwin a solid background in what we would today call life science and Earth science.

Darwin's training, and the contacts he made at school, came together in one of the most fateful first-job offers ever extended to a recent college graduate. One of Darwin's Cambridge professors arranged to have him be the resident naturalist aboard the HMS Beagle. This was a ship that was to undertake a survey of coastal areas around the world. In addition to numerous stops on the east coast of South America (the ship's primary survey site), the Beagle also stopped briefly at the remote Galapagos Islands, about nine hundred seventy kilometers or six hundred miles west of Ecuador.

Thus did Darwin spend time on a research vessel—five years in all—beginning in England two days after Christmas 1831 and ending back there in October 1836. Just twenty-two when he left, he was prone to seasickness; he had to share a 10-by-15-foot room with two other officers; he was not a traveler by nature; and the journey was dangerous. Three of the Beagle's officers died because of illness during the journey. Yet Darwin was happy because of the work he was doing: looking, listening, collecting, and thinking about it all. (Adapted from Krogh, David, Biology a Guide to the Natural World, 2nd ed. Upper Saddle River, N.J: Prentice Hall, 2002. 324–325)

11. The first paragraph is organized by

   a. definition order.
   b. sequence/process order.
   c. sequence/chronological order.
   d. contrast order.

12. The second paragraph is organized by

   a. cause and effect order.
   b. sequence/process order.
   c. classification order.
   d. contrast order.

13. According to the passage, Darwin was happiest when he was studying

   a. to be a doctor.
   b. divinity.
   c. nature.
   d. at the University of Edinburgh.

14. According to the passage Darwin

   a. was offered a job on the HMS Beagle because of his divinity degree.
   b. was offered a position on the HMS Beagle because of his skills and because he knew people at school who could help him.
   c. received the offer for the position on the HMS Beagle because of his medical training at the University of Edinburgh.
   d. received the job offer on the HMS Beagle because his father had contacts and Darwin had medical and divinity skills learned at Cambridge and the University of Edinburgh.

Passage Six

Hypnosis is a set of attention-focusing procedures in which changes in a person's behavior or state of mind are suggested. In one form or another, hypnosis has been around for centuries. But the earliest known reference to it is traced to Franz Anton Mesmer (1734-1815), a Viennese physician. Mesmer believed that illness was caused by an imbalance of magnetic fluids in the body—and could be cured by restoring the proper balance. Working in Paris, he would pass his hands across the patient's body and wave a magnetic wand over the infected area. Many patients would descend into a trance and then awaken feeling better. The medical community, however, viewed this treatment with skepticism, and in 1784 a French commission chaired by Benjamin Franklin found that there was no scientific basis for the "animal Magnetism" theory, only "mere imagination." Mesmer was called a quack and run out of town. When he died, he was penniless. Yet to this day, we acknowledge his work whenever we describe ourselves as being mesmerized. (Kassin, Saul, Psychology, 3rd ed. . Upper Saddle River, N.J: Prentice Hall, 2001. 155.)

15. According to the passage,

    a. Franz Mesmer experienced some success in his career.
    b. Franz Mesmer was a quack.
    c. Benjamin Franklin was a supporter of Franz Mesmer's ideas.
    d. the medical community viewed Mesmer's treatments with enthusiasm.

Details and Logical Patterns Test 2

Read the passages and answer the questions.

Passage One

        Boys and girls alike crawl, walk, and smile to about the same age, and both become curious about sex in adolescence. Similarly, both men and women see better in daylight than in the dark, fall prey to optical illusion, and behave in ways that bring reward. Both men and women can hold about seven items in short-term memory, use shorthand cognitive heuristics in making judgments, and affiliate with others in times of stress. In their social behavior, both men and women are biased by their first impressions, are attracted to others who are similar, and are more likely to help others when they're alone than in a group of bystanders. The list of similarities that escape our daily notice is long and impressive. As human beings, men and women are more alike than different in many "invisible" ways. (Kassin, Saul, Psychology, 3rd ed. Upper Saddle River, N.J: Prentice Hall, 2001. 561.)

1. The author uses an overall organizational pattern of

    a. simple listing.
    b. process.
    c. cause effect.
    d. comparison and contrast.

2. According to the passage,

    a. men are more helpful to others when they are in a group.
    b. women and men are more helpful to others when they are with a friend.
    c. men and women are more likely to help others when they are alone.
    d. men and women affiliate with others in order to help others who are in trouble.

3. What logical thinking pattern signal words are used in this paragraph to signal the pattern?

    a. crawl, walk, smile, hold, see, are biased, are attracted
    b. alike, similarities, both, similarly
    c. list, alone, group
    d. affiliate, bystanders, impressions.

Passage Two

        In contrast to major depression, a unipolar disorder in which moods range from neutral to depressed, bipolar disorder produces wild fluctuations that range from manic (a euphoric, overactive state) to depressed (a state of hopelessness and apathy). In what used to be called "manic-depression," bipolar-disorder patients alternate uncontrollably between the two extremes, in cycles that last from a few days to several months. One week, they are flying as high as a kite, bursting with energy and optimism. The next week, they have sunk to the depths of despair. (Kassin, Saul, Psychology, 3rd ed. Upper Saddle River, N.J: Prentice Hall, 2001. 649.)

4. For this paragraph, the author uses an overall organizational pattern of

   a. simple listing.
   b. definition.
   c. cause effect.
   d. comparison and contrast.

5. According to the passage,

   a. major depression and bipolar-disorder are the same disorder.
   b. major depression patients alternate uncontrollably between the two extremes of manic and depressed.
   c. bipolar-disorder patients have moods that go from neutral to manic.
   d. bipolar-disorder patients have moods that range from manic to depressed.

6. Which type of details are the last two sentences?

   a. facts
   b. descriptions
   c. examples
   d. references

Passage Three

Just outside of Cairo, Egypt, is a famous plateau called Giza. This is the home of the Great Pyramids, the only surviving entry on the list of the Seven Wonders of the Ancient World. There are three types of pyramids at Giza. The largest, and oldest, was built as the tomb of the Pharaoh Khufu around 2550 B.C. This pyramid is made from over 2,300,000 blocks of stone weighing a total of 6.5 million tons. It took about 30 years to build this monument. Prior to the 20th century, Khufu's pyramid was the tallest building in the world. Khufu's son Khafre is responsible for the second-largest pyramid at Giza during his rule as pharaoh between 2520 to 2494 B.C. The smallest of the pyramids at Giza is credited to Menkaure, believed to be the son of Khafre and grandson of Khufe. (Martin-Gay, K. Elayn, Basic College Mathematics, 2nd ed. Upper Saddle River, N.J: Prentice Hall, 2003. 467.)

7. What types of details are in the paragraph?

   a. facts
   b. examples
   c. descriptions
   d. definitions

8. According to the passage, the largest pyramid on the Giza plateau was the tomb of

   a. Pharaoh Khafre.
   b. Pharaoh Menkaura.
   c. Pharaoh Giza.
   d. Pharaoh Khufu.

Passage Four

A tornado is a violent, whirling column of air that is often spawned by the unstable weather conditions that occur during thunderstorms. Although tornadoes are capable of sustaining wind speeds of 250 to more than 300 mph, most tornadoes have wind speeds under 110 mph. The average forward speed of a tornado is 30 mph, but some tornadoes have been known to travel over land at speeds up to 70 mph. The path of a tornado can extend anywhere from a few feet to 100 miles long. Each year in the United States, an average of 800 tornadoes occur, causing an average of 80 deaths. The deadliest tornado in the United States was the Tri-State Tornado Outbreak on March 18, 1925, which killed 689 people and injured over 2000 more in Missouri, Illinois, and Indiana. (Martin-Gay, K. Elayn, Basic College Mathematics, 2nd ed. Upper Saddle River, N.J: Prentice Hall, 2003. 549)

9. For this passage, the author uses an overall organizational pattern of

   a. simple listing.
   b. Definition.
   c. cause and effect.
   d. comparison and contrast.

10. According to the passage, tornadoes usually have a land speed around _____ miles per hour.

   a. 30
   b. 250
   c. 100
   d. 300

Passage Five

If problems are viewed as barriers or blocks, they can become a source of inconvenience, annoyance, and failure. If you view problems as those things that prevent you from having a happy and productive life, it indicates that your goal is to completely eliminate problems. Unfortunately, this is an impossible goal. A more constructive view is that problems exist for a purpose and that they present an opportunity to actively participate in life. Your goals should include actively confronting problems, working toward personally meaningful resolutions, and generating creative options to deal with problems as they arise. (Nelson, Darwin B. and Low, Gary R. Emotional Intelligence Achieving Academic and Career Excellence, Upper Saddle River, N.J: Prentice Hall, 2003. 75.)

11. Which type of logical thinking pattern is used in this paragraph?

   a. cause and effect order
   b. sequence/chronological order
   c. classification order
   d. listing order

12. According to this passage, what is an impossible goal?

   a. Your goal to actively deal with problems as they occur.
   b. Your goal to work toward personally meaningful resolutions.
   c. Your goal to completely do away with problems.
   d. Your goal to view problems as an inconvenience.

Passage Six

   Sculpture is categorized according to whether it is carved or modeled and whether it is a relief or freestanding. Relief remains tied to the background, from which it only partially emerges, in contrast to freestanding sculpture, which is fully liberated from it. A further distinction is made between low relief and high relief, depending on how much the carving projects. However, since scale as well as depth must be taken into account, there is no single guideline, so that a third category, middle relief, is sometimes cited. (Janson, H.W. and Janson, Anthony F. A Basic History of Art, 6th ed. Upper Saddle River, N.J: Prentice Hall, 2003.29)

13. Which type of logical thinking pattern is used in this paragraph?

   a. cause and effect order
   b. sequence/chronological order
   c. classification order
   d. listing order

14. What types of details are in the paragraph?

   a. facts
   b. examples
   c. descriptions
   d. definitions

15. According to the paragraph, there are _____ types of relief.

   a. 5
   b. 4
   c. 3
   d. 2

Answer Key Test 1

1. b
2. d
3. b
4. d

5. b
6. a
7. c
8. d
9. d
10. a
11. c
12. a
13. c
14. b
15. a

Answer Key Test 2

1. d
2. b
3. d
4. c
5. a
6. d
7. c
8. a
9. d
10. b
11. a
12. c
13. c
14. c
15. d

Chapter Eight: Graphic Aids

Summary

Authors often use visuals called graphic aids to support the ideas presented in the text, show relationships between the ideas, state details, and to help readers to understand. Visuals attract readers and make the information easier to understand. To understand graphic aids readers must use many of the same methods that work with texts or informational material.

Graphic aids can help readers to understand the material they are reading when the reader is able to associate the material in the visual with the text in the reading. There are three elements to look for when you are looking at a graphic aid. They are the topic, the main idea, and the details. After the reader has located this information it is important to associate it with the text and comprehend it. Then the readers should apply the information to their lives or to those around them, and lastly consider how the information compares and contrasts with other knowledge they possess, how the information relates to other knowledge they posses, and draw conclusions about the information.

There are five basic forms of graphic aids. They are bar graphs, line graphs, pie charts, tables, and diagrams. Each type of visual aid signals a particular relationship between the types of data included on the graphic aid. Each graphic aid should be analyzed in a specific manner.

Line graphs show how two sets of material are related. To make conclusions about the information, the reader must read the graph carefully and figure out what numbers would correspond to the spot on the graph being considered.

Bar graphs show differences between groups. There are two types of bar graphs. When the reader is considering a single bar graph, they will need to figure out what number the top of the bar represents. When the bar graph contains a stacked bar graph, it may be necessary to add the parts together before making comparisons and contrasts.

Pie charts present the information by using a circular diagram, which is divided up to show proportions of a whole. This type of graph is used when authors want to show what percentage of a group has particular characteristic. It is important to note the titles and labels as well as any text presented in order to understand the information presented by this graph. Think about the relationship of each part to the whole. It is sometimes necessary to add a few parts together to answer a question.

It is not necessary to analyze all tables because some of them are presentations of knowledge in a condensed form. It is important to note the categories and subcategories. For numeric tables, it may be necessary to consider differences and to compare and contrast the information found within the table.

Diagrams are drawings to give the reader visualizations of the material presented by the author. They are used to simplify the information and to make it easier for the reader to understand. It is important to note in what order the information should be viewed and where parts are located. Labels and arrows should be considered.

Graphic information can help the reader understand the ideas more easily. It is important to carefully look at the graphics that are provided by the author.

Teaching Tips:

- It is important to use visuals to show the students examples of each type of graph or table.

- It would be helpful to create graphs with information that is related to the students. Associations with life help students to remember the information.

Suggested Activities:

- Write an entry explaining why graphs can sometimes make information more understandable.

- Create a pie graph showing how they would divide the 168 hours in a week. Remind them to include their classes, work time, study time (about two hours for each hour in class), and leisure activities.

- Ask the group to answer questions that compare and contrast information such as, "Who likes cats better than dogs?", and "Who likes dogs better than cats?" Ask additional questions that you could contrast in a bar graph. Make a double bar graph to chart the results of one contrasting question. Assign small groups to create a double bar graph using the results of the various questions. Have the students write one or two question to go with their graph. Encourage them to make the questions challenging by asking about percentages or fractions. Switch papers and have the other group answer the questions.

- Have each student find a graph in a magazine, on the web, or in a newspaper. Have the student mount the graph on a large index card. Have each student create three questions about their graph. Collect the graphs and number the cards. Have the students get into groups of three. Pass each group take three cards with the graphs and the questions. Have each group label their paper with the numbers of the cards they received and answer the questions on their card. Have each group switch cards with another group and have the new group correct the answers from the first group.

Graphic Aids Test 1

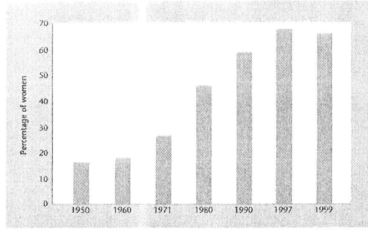

Percentage of women recipients of PhDs in psychology, 1950-1999.
Source: Summary Report: Doctorate Recipients from United States Universities (Selected Years). National Research Council. Figure compiled by the APA Research Office. Copyright © 2000. 1999 data from the National Science Foundation. 2002.

1. What percentage of women received Ph.D.s in 1971?

   a. 20
   b. 30
   c. 27
   d. 8

2. What trend is noticeable?

    a. people are receiving more doctorates
    b. people are receiving less Ph.D.s
    c. women are receiving more doctorates
    d. women are receiving less Ph.D.s

3. Women who participated in the study received their

    a. doctorates worldwide.
    b. doctorates in the U.S.
    c. Ph.D.s in Europe.
    d. Ph.D.s in APA.

4. The percentage of women receiving their doctorates increased by what percentage from 1950 to 1980?

    a. 20%
    b. 28%
    c. 14%
    d. 35%

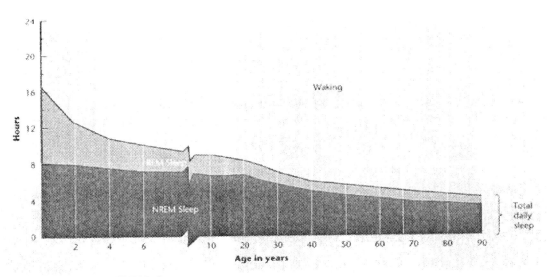

Changes in REM and NREM sleep.
Source: Adapted with permission from H.P. Roffwarg. "Ontogenetic Development of the Human Sleep-Dream Cycle," Science, 152, p. 604. Copyright © 1966 by the American Association for the Advancement of Science.

5. The total daily sleep a six year old needs is about

    a. 8 hours.
    b. 11 hours.
    c. 6 hours.
    d. 13 hours.

6. Adults that are 55 need

   a. less than 2 hours REM sleep.
   b. about 6 hours REM sleep.
   c. more than 6 hours NREM sleep.
   d. less than 5 hours NREM sleep.

7. A new baby needs

   a. about equal amounts of REM and NREM sleep.
   b. 8 hours of REM sleep.
   c. 16 hours of NREM sleep.
   d. 22 hours of REM and NREM sleep.

8. A 40 year old needs _____ NREM sleep than a 90 year old.

   a. 2 times as much
   b. 1.5 times as much
   c. 4 hours less
   d. 1 hour less

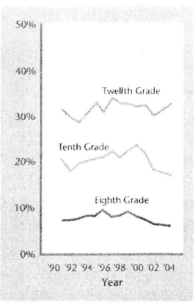

Teenage use of alcohol (% drunk in past 30 days.)
Source: L.D. Johnston, P.M. O'Malley, J.G. Bachmann, & Schulenberg. (2005).
Monitoring the Future national results on adolescent drug use: Overview of key findings. 2004.
(NIH Publication No. 05-5726). Bethesda, MD: National Institute on Drug Abuse.

9. The use of alcohol by teenagers from 1990 to 2002 has

   a. remained the same.
   b. decreased noticeably.
   c. decreased slightly.
   d. increased slightly.

10. The researchers for this study published the results _____ the NIH Publicity of the Key Findings.

    a. before
    b. after
    c. at the same time as
    d. 2 years later

11. Which grades had a significant gain in alcohol consumption from 1998-1999?

    a. 12th and 10th
    b. 12th and 8th
    c. 8th and 10th
    d. all the grades

12. Which grade shower the greatest decline from 2000 to 2002?

    a. 10
    b. 12
    c. 8
    d. all of the above

Levels of Alcohol in the Blood	Behavioral Effects
0.05%	Feels good; less alert
0.10%	Slower to react; less cautious
0.15%	Reaction time much slower
0.20%	Sensory-motor abilities suppressed
0.25%	Staggering(motor abilities severely impaired); perception is limited as well
0.30%	Semistupor
0.35%	Level for anesthesia
0.40%	Death is likely (usually as a result of respiratory failure)

The Behavioral Effects of Blood Alcohol Levels
Source: Data from Drugs, Society, and Human Behavior, 10th ed., by Oakley Ray, 2003, New York: McGraw-Hill: U.S. National Library of Medicine. (2006). *Alcohol Use*. Retrieved March 16, 2006, from http://www.nlm.nih.gov/medlineplus/ency/article/001944.htm.

13. At what level of alcohol in the blood would your eyesight become affected?

    a. .05%
    b. .10%
    c. .15%
    d. .20%

14. What is the major cause of death among people who consume great amounts of alcohol?

    a. heart attack
    b. blood vessels in the stomach bursting
    c. anesthesia
    d. respiratory failure

15. At which level of alcohol in the blood would people face the possibility of death?

    a. .30%
    b. .35%
    c. .40%
    d. .10%

Graphic Aids Test 2

Levels of Alcohol in the Blood	Behavioral Effects
0.05%	Feels good; less alert
0.10%	Slower to react; less cautious
0.15%	Reaction time much slower
0.20%	Sensory-motor abilities suppressed
0.25%	Staggering(motor abilities severely impaired); perception is limited as well
0.30%	Semistupor
0.35%	Level for anesthesia
0.40%	Death is likely (usually as a result of respiratory failure)

The Behavioral Effects of Blood Alcohol Levels
Source: Data from Drugs, Society, and Human Behavior, 10th ed., by Oakley Ray. 2003. New York: McGraw-Hill; U.S. National Library of Medicine. (2006). *Alcohol Use*. Retrieved March 16, 2006, from http://www.nlm.nih.gov/medlineplus/ency/article/001944.htm.

1. Why do many states set the DUI levels at less than .10%?

    a. People are feeling too good to drive correctly.
    b. People's reaction time is slower.
    c. People's eyesight is affected.
    d. People cannot control their motor ability.

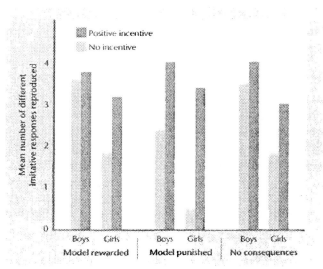

Results of Bandura's Study
Source: A. Bandura. Influence of models' reinforcement contingencies on rthe acquisition of initative responses. Journal of Personlaity and Social Psychologyu. 1. 592. 1965. APA

2. What kind of imitative response was Bandura tracking?

   a. passive
   b. aggressive
   c. students' response to personal rewards
   d. students' response to personal punishment

3. When the models were rewarded, boys increased their mean imitative responses by _____ when a positive incentive was added.

   a. about 3 responses
   b. about 2 responses
   c. about 1 response
   d. less than ½ response

4. When the models were rewarded, girls increased their mean imitative responses by _____ when a positive incentive was added

   a. about 3.5 responses
   b. about 2.5 responses
   c. about 1.5 responses
   d. less than .5 responses

5. Girls responded to the models similarly when the model was

   a. rewarded with no incentive and the model was given no consequence and no incentive.
   b. rewarded with a positive incentive and the model was given a consequence.
   c. given no incentive and the model was given an incentive.
   d. given no consequence and the model was given a positive incentive.

6. In which group did the greatest change occur between models with positive incentives and models with no incentive?

   a. boys with the model rewarded for aggressive behavior
   b. girls with the model rewarded for aggressive behavior
   c. boys with the model punished for aggressive behavior
   d. girls with the model punished for aggressive behavior

7. The mean number of responses of different imitative responses reproduced was the same for which categories of boys?

   a. model rewarded with a positive incentive and no consequence with a positive incentive
   b. model punished with a positive incentive and no consequences with a positive incentive
   c. model rewarded with a positive incentive and no consequences with a positive incentive
   d. model punished with no incentive and no consequence with no consequence and no incentive

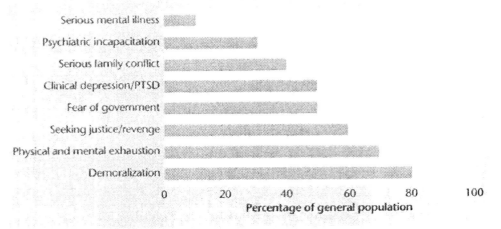

Mental trauma in societies at war.
Source. Mollica. R.F. (2000 June). Invisible wounds. *Scientific American*. p. 54. Figure by Laurie Grace.

8. The three psychological reactions that occurred in more than 50% of the population of societies at war were

   a. clinical depression; fear of government; seek justice and revenge.
   b. seeking justice and revenge; physical and mental exhaustion; clinical depression.
   c. seeking justice and revenge; physical and mental exhaustion; demoralization.
   d. demoralization; fear of government; and physical and mental exhaustion.

9. Which two psychological reactions occur at about the same rate?

   a. demoralization and physical and mental exhaustion
   b. clinical depression and fear of government
   c. serious family conflict and psychiatric incapacitations
   d. fear of government and serious family conflict

10. Demoralization due to war occurs in how much greater percentage that serious family conflict due to war?

   a. 40%
   b. 30%
   c. 20%
   d. 10%

11. How many categories of psychological reactions did the researchers study?

   a. 9
   b. 7
   c. 8
   d. 6

Answer Key Test 1

1. c
2. c
3. b
4. b
5. a
6. a
7. a
8. b
9. b
10. b
11. c
12. a
13. d
14. d
15. b

Answer Key Test 2

1. b
2. b
3. d
4. c
5. a
6. d
7. b
8. c
9. b
10. a
11. c

Chapter Nine: Drawing Conclusions

Summary

There is more to understanding the meaning of a paragraph or a passage than just the words you see on the page. Feeling, thought, reasoning, and judgment are all part of comprehending the message that is being conveyed. Drawing conclusions is essential to understanding more of what you read. In order to draw more accurate conclusions from what you read, you need to be aware of the different levels of comprehension known as literal, inferential, and critical.

Literal or basic comprehension is the factual or direct account of what is stated on a page. Literal questions can be answered by finding the actual words written on a page that can be used to answer a particular question. Inferential reading refers to the message that is implied in the paragraph, passage, or story. This level of reading requires the reader to use suggestions made by the author in order to determine what is being stated. Critical comprehension requires the reader to analyze and evaluate a message. Being able to critically examine what you read depends primarily on your ability to make inferences and draw conclusions. Distinguishing between these varying levels of comprehension will enable you to become a more skilled reader.

Additionally, understanding the author's purpose, the author's tone, and being able to distinguish between fact and opinion will help you grasp not only what the author is saying, but also what he is not saying.

The author's purpose is the objective that the writer wants to achieve. There are three general purposes: to inform, entertain, and persuade. To determine an author's purpose, readers need to identify what the author is emphasizing and then draw conclusions based on what he or she thinks the purpose may be.

The author's tone is the author's attitude toward a subject. To determine tone critical readers examine the language used by the author, looking closely at the difference between connotative and denotative. Connotative meaning is the emotional meaning that a word suggests. Denotative meaning is the accepted definition of a term.

An author can influence both a reader's beliefs and opinions. Distinguishing facts from opinions enables the reader to make inferences. Information that can be proven to be true or false is fact. For facts to be considered good support, they must be true, current, relevant, and reliable. Opinion is a person's judgment about people, places, or things. For an opinion to be convincing, it must be reasonable, relevant, useful, and well supported with details.

Making inferences requires a reader to figure out an unstated message. When we interpret what an author implies we are drawing inferences. These implications are based on how you infer the author's purpose and tone, as well as any points that the author implies.

In reading articles and essays, critical readers analyze the structure of the content and then evaluate the merits of the message. Articles give the reader a report of an event, situation, or new discovery. Articles have four structural elements: the headline, lead, development, and conclusion. An essay is an expository text in which the author expresses his or her personal ideas or experiences. It has five structural elements: the title, introduction, thesis, body paragraphs, topic sentences, and conclusion. Readers can use the first five steps in PDQ3R to analyze the structural elements in both articles and essays and then evaluate the qualities of the points during the review step.

Teaching Tips:

- Stress the following points to your students to help them make inferences and draw conclusions. First, make sure that the inferences and conclusions you draw are based on facts. Next, use the information that you know and the experiences that you have had to help you determine inferences and conclusions. Lastly, consider all the facts and all the possible explanations in a situation before making an inference or drawing a conclusion.

- Recognizing and understanding the meaning of several types of figurative language will help students draw inferences. Explain how figurative language helps readers make inferences about comparisons that are not literally true and sometimes not logically related. Show students examples of how figurative language can be used with words to change meaning in context.

Listed below are five different types of figurative language:

Metaphors: A metaphor is a figure of speech which directly compares two unlike things. This comparison is done without using the words "like" or "as."

> Example: Lisa's stare was icy cold.

Similes: A simile is a figure of speech which directly compares two unlike things using the words "like" or "as."

> Example: The students were as noisy and restless as animals trying to get out of a cage.

Verbal Irony: Verbal irony is a figure of speech that uses words to say one thing, but you really mean the opposite of what is said.

> Example: Yesterday was truly a wonderful day; it was raining, the wind was blowing and I had a flat tire on my way to work.

Personification: Personification is a figure of speech that gives human characteristics to nonhuman objects.

> Example: The wind howled, and the rain pounded against the house.

Idioms: An idiom is a figure of speech that does not make sense literally, but because it has been used over the years, it has taken on its own meaning and is accepted and used in the English language.

> Example: John could not eat all of the food he put on his plate; the selections on the table were so varied, his eyes became bigger than his stomach.

Suggested Activities:

- Have students find two examples of idioms. Ask them to bring their examples to class. Put students in pairs and have them read their idioms to each other. Ask each pair of students to record whether or not their partner understood the meaning of each idiom. After the student pairs determine which idioms their partners do not understand, ask the students to write those idioms on the board. Discuss the meanings of the idioms that are on the board. Discuss how figures of speech have changed over time, and why it is so difficult for students whose first language is not English to understand the meaning of idioms.

- Have students select an editorial cartoon from a newspaper or magazine. Ask them to review the piece they selected and come up with two questions relating to inference and drawing conclusions. Next, put students in pairs to discuss their questions. Lastly, ask each pair of students to collaborate on a paragraph summary of what they learned from this activity.

- Have students cut paragraphs from magazines or newspapers and mount the paragraphs on index cards. Collect the cards and put them in a pile. Divide the class into groups of four. Pass out four cards to each group. Have each student read one paragraph with tone and have the other students in the group identify the tone. Finally, have the students decide if the reader used the appropriate tone.

- Select an editorial from a newspaper or magazine. Make copies of the editorial for each student in your class. Ask each student to find at least two sentences in the editorial that are fact and two sentences that are opinion. Ask them how they distinguished the differences between the sentences. Ask some students to write their sentences on the board and discuss them with the class.

Drawing Conclusions Test 1

Read the following passages and choose the statement that best expresses the most logical inference or conclusion that can be reached based on the information provided in the passage.

Passage One

The public's view of heroes in the United States has changed throughout the last century. In past centuries, many countries' military leaders or religious figures such as Joan of Arc were regarded as heroes. During World War I and World War II in the twentieth century, members of the military in our country were viewed as heroes.

But as radio, movies, and television became commonplace in United States during the last hundred years, the heroes changed to entertainment and sports stars. In the later part of the twentieth century and the beginning of the twenty-first century, many people looked to stars, such as Jesse Ventura or Britney Spears, to help them choose their values. Children modeled their behavior after cartoon characters. The Ninja Turtles, Mighty Mouse, and Power Rangers became heroes to children because they saved characters on the shows. However, something happened during the fall in 2001 that changed the type of heroes people in the United States admired. After the attack on the World Trade Center, people began to regard firemen and policemen as heroes because they exposed their lives to danger or sacrificed their lives while they were attempting to save others. (Some of the information and ideas in this paragraph have been adapted from Macionis, John J. Sociology. 9th ed. Upper Saddle Ridge, NJ: Prentice Hall, 2003. p. 72)

1. A conclusion that can be drawn from this passage is that

   a. radio, movies, and television have propelled entertainment and sports stars into the limelight over the last hundred years.
   b. the attack on the World Trade Center changed the way fireman and policemen do their jobs.
   c. over the past century, people in the United States have changed their views about heroes.
   d. children model their behavior after cartoon characters.

2. What does the following sentence from the passage suggest about radio, movies, and television?

But as radio, movies, and television became commonplace in United States during the last hundred years, the heroes changed to entertainment and sports stars.

   a. Radio, television, and movies are all very popular with people in the United States.
   b. Radio, television, and movies are something people in the United States take for granted.
   c. In the last century, radio, movies, and television have been responsible for changing the way people in the United States define heroes.
   d. Entertainment and sports stars have become heroes because of radio, movies, and television.

After the attack on the World Trade Center, people began to regard firemen and policemen as heroes because they exposed their lives to danger or sacrificed their lives while they were attempting to save others.

3. The above sentence is a statement of

   a. fact.
   b. opinion.

Passage Two

Until 2002, major television networks in the United States either portrayed minorities in a stereotypical manner or rarely included them in shows and movies, and this needed to be changed. The major networks offered few choices of family shows with minorities, but more minorities were being included in major network shows set in employment settings. Shows such as Third Watch, Cops, and E.R. had some minority characters, but they were not in the forefront of the show weekly as a major character on a sitcom might be. Other shows did include minorities such as homosexuals, but the characters still followed the old stereotypes. In many cartoons even the animals, such as cats, were treated stereotypically; Tom and Jerry was a good example of this treatment. Some of the smaller networks carried some shows, like My Wife and Kids, that featured minority characters in family situations that more closely depicted people in semi-realistic settings, but the major networks rarely followed their example. Some of the popular shows, Frazier and Friends, rarely included minorities in their shows. As a result, many people thought it would be good for the major television networks to include characters from more minority groups and to have the situations in the shows represent these characters at least as realistically as others in different shows were portrayed. (Some information and ideas in this paragraph have been adapted from Macionis, John J. Sociology, 9th ed. Upper Saddle River, NJ: Prentice Hall, 2003. p. 128)

4. A conclusion that can be drawn from this passage is that

   a. major television networks should include characters from more minority groups.
   b. in many cartoons, animals are treated stereotypically.
   c. a lot of people watch the television shows Frazier and Friends.
   d. until a couple of years ago, major television networks in the U.S. portrayed minorities in a stereotypical way.

5. What does the following sentence from the passage suggest about major television networks?

Until 2002, major television networks in the United States either portrayed minorities in a stereotypical manner or rarely included them in shows and movies, and this needed to be changed.

    a. Major television networks in the United States have a prejudice against minorities.
    b. Minorities on television shows in the United States are portrayed in a stereotypical manner.
    c. After 2002, major television networks in the United States began changing the way minorities were portrayed in television shows.
    d. Major television networks did not include very many minorities in shows and movies before the year 2002, and when minorities were included they were portrayed in a stereotypical manner.

6. As a result, many people thought it would be good for the major television networks to include characters from more minority groups and to have the situations in the shows represent these characters at least as realistically as others in different shows were portrayed.

The above sentence is a statement of

    a. fact.
    b. opinion.

Passage Three

       Chemists of the eighteenth and nineteenth centuries developed flame tests that used the coleus of flames to identify several elements. Sodium salts give the persistent yellow flame, potassium salts a fleeting lavender and lithium salts a brilliant red flame. Like those of fireworks, these flame colors result from the electron structures of atoms of the specific elements.
       Fireworks originated earlier than flame tests, in ancient China. The brilliant colors of aerial displays still mark our celebrations of patriotic holidays. The colors of fireworks are attributed to specific elements. Brilliant reds are produced by strontium compounds, whereas barium compounds give yellow-green, sodium compounds yield yellow, and copper salts produce a greenish blue.
       The colors of fireworks and flame tests are not what they seem to the unaided eye. If the light from the flame is passed through a prism, it is separated into light of several different colors. (Hill, John W. and Kolb, Doris K. Chemistry for Changing Times, 10th ed. Upper Saddle River Road, N.J: Prentice Hall. 2004. pgs. 68-69.)

7. A conclusion that can be drawn from this passage is that

    a. fireworks originated earlier than flame tests.
    b. the brilliant colors given off by flames and fireworks are attributed to specific elements.
    c. sodium salts, potassium salts, and lithium salts give off persistent yellow, fleeting lavender, and brilliant red flames.
    d. the brilliant colors of aerial displays still mark our celebrations of patriotic holidays.

The colors of fireworks and flame tests are not what they seem to the unaided eye.

8. The above sentence is a statement of

    a. fact.
    b. opinion.

Passage Four

The act of hearing isn't quite the same as the act of listening. While hearing refers to sensing spoken messages from their source, listening involves a complex process of communication. Successful listening occurs when the speaker's intended message reaches the listener. In school and at home, poor listening may cause communication breakdowns and mistakes. Skilled listening, however, promotes progress and success. Listening is a teachable—and learnable—skill.

Ralph G. Nichols, a pioneer in listening research, studied 200 students at the University of Minnesota over a nine-month period. His findings demonstrate that effective listening depends as much on positive attitude as on specific skills. Just as understanding the mind actions involved in critical thinking help you work out problems, understanding the listening process helps you become a better listener. (Carter, Carol, Bishop, Joyce and Kravits, Sarah Lyman Keys to success in College, Career, and Life. 4th ed. Upper Saddle River, NJ: Prentice Hall, 2003. 193)

9. What is the overall tone of this passage?

   a. sentimental
   b. defiant
   c. humorous
   d. encouraging

10. Listening is a teachable and learnable skill.

   The above sentence is a statement of

   a. fact.
   b. opinion.

Read the statements below and determine the author's purpose by labeling them as entertaining, informative, or persuasive. Place an E in front of entertaining statements, an I before informative statements, and a P before persuasive statements.

_____1. The frontal lobe of the brain is located at the front of the skull behind your forehead; this section processes voluntary muscle movement and manages planning and organizing our expressive behavior.

_____2. After 2002, major television networks in the United States began changing the way minorities were portrayed in television shows.

_____3. My friend has faithfully worked for our government for twenty-five years, and he deserves some compensation for his loyalty to his country.

_____4. Ten thousand fringed, tie-dyed, jeaned, and cotton-draped bodies crammed into the football field facing the gargantuan speakers and stage on the twentieth yard line.

_____5. Major television networks should include characters from more minority groups and should have the situations in the shows represent these characters at least as realistically as others in different shows were portrayed.

Drawing Conclusions Test 2

Read the following passages and choose the statement that best expresses the most logical inference or conclusion that can be reached based on the information provided in the passage.

Passage One

One of the primary differences between ancient Mesopotamia and Egypt was Egypt's political stability. Mesopotamian cultures came and went, some growing into powerful empires while others were relatively short-lived. Egypt, however, maintained its cultural community for around 3000 years (roughly from 3100 B.C. until the Roman conquest in 31 B.C.). This was possible in large part because Egypt's social and political structures were more easily controlled than those of Mesopotamia.

Egypt was also more geographically isolated and unified than Mesopotamia. Located in northeast Africa, Egypt was separated from the rest of the Ancient Near East and protected by its geographical boundaries—the Mediterranean Sea in the north, the first cataract of the Nile in the south, desert and Sinai Peninsular in the east, and the Sahara in the west—which made Egypt less open to foreign invasion than Mesopotamia. The country itself was united by the Nile, which at 4160 miles is the longest river in the world. Although less than 1000 miles of the Nile is in Egypt.

Egypt also had its own writing system, called "the gods' words" by Egyptians, which differed from Mesopotamian cuneiform. Egyptians used the more pictorial hieroglyphs (literally "sacred carvings") for official and religious texts and a simple cursive script called hieratic, derived from hieroglyphs. Because scholars can now read both hieroglyphs and hieratic, a great deal is known about ancient Egyptian culture. (Adams, Schneider Adams, Exploring the Humanities: Creativity and Culture in the West, Upper Saddle Ridge, NJ: Prentice Hall, 2006. p. 41)

1. A conclusion that can be drawn from this passage is that

    a. Mesopotamian cultures came and went, but the Egyptian culture was more stable.
    b. Egypt was more protected by its geographical boundaries than Mesopotamia.
    c. a great deal more is known today about the ancient Egyptian culture because Egypt's social and political structures were more easily controlled than those of Mesopotamia.
    d. Egypt was a better place to live than Mesopotamia.

2. What do the following sentences from the passage suggest about Egyptian and Mesopotamian cultures.

    Mesopotamian cultures came and went, some growing into powerful empires while others were relatively short-lived. Egypt, however, maintained its cultural community for around 3000 years (roughly from 3100 B.C. until the Roman conquest in 31 B.C.).

    a. The Egyptian culture was better than the Mesopotamian culture.
    b. The people who lived in Mesopotamia envied the people who lived in Egypt.
    c. Mesopotamian culture was more not as stable as Egyptian culture.
    d. The Egyptian culture was destroyed by the Romans in 31 B.C.

3. What is the overall tone of this passage?

    a. informative
    b. defiant
    c. straightforward
    d. critical

4. One of the primary differences between ancient Mesopotamia and Egypt was Egypt's political stability.

    The above sentence is a statement of

    a. fact.
    b. opinion.

5. Many scholars think that the Egyptian culture created a better system of writing than the culture of Mesopotamia.

    The above sentence is a statement of

    a. fact.
    b. opinion.

Passage Two

One of the most famous of the cromlechs, a monumental stone structure made of huge blocks of boulders used singly or in groups, that was used for religious rites is Stonehenge in Southern England. What we see today is the result of several distinct building campaigns, beginning in the New Stone Age and continuing into the early Bronze Age. During the first phase, from roughly 3500 to 2900 B.C., a nearly continuous circle was dug into the chalk ground. A silted ditch was added about 3300-2140 B.C. and then the avenue down to the Avon River sometime from 2580 to 1890 B.C. The sandstone circle of evenly spaced trilithons, each consisting of two upright posts and a horizontal slab, was erected during the early Bronze Age Wessex culture between 2850 and 2200 B.C. These immense stones were evidently dragged from Marlborough Downs, some twenty miles away—a feat as awesome as raising them, but it is a far from clear whether the inner bluestone circle and horseshoe, which date from several hundred years later (2480-1940 B.C.), were deposited by glaciers or carried by carts and rafts from the Preseli Mountains in Wales some two hundred miles to the west. During the final phase, from 2030 to 1520 B.C., this arrangement was echoed in two similarly marked circles and a smaller horseshoe that enclose an altar like stone at the center.

Why was Stonehenge built in the first place? The widely held belief that the so-called Heel Stone was positioned so that the sun would rise directly above it on the day of the summer solstice, when the sun is farthest from the equator, has long been shown to be incorrect. It appears that Stonehenge was originally aligned with the major and minor moonrises. Only later, did the structure become oriented toward the sun; the Heel Stone and fallen "Slaughter Stone," along with other stones and the alignment of the causeway were rearranged in the direction of the summer sunrise.

Each of Stonehenge's building phases was linked to broader changes during the Neolithic and Bronze Ages. Burial mounds and prehistoric monuments made of circles of massive stones from as early as 3500 B.C. that have been found in Scandinavia and northern Britain reflect the changeover to a settled, agrarian way of life. However, the people who created the Wessex culture probably crossed the English Channel from Brittany in northwestern France, where massive horseshoes made of enormous stones constructed with astronomical arrangements are far more common than in England. They brought with them Bronze Age technologies and ideas that must have seemed revolutionary to the local population, who initially put up a stiff resistance. In Stonehenge and elsewhere in southern England, these newcomers imposed their own traditions on established practices. In addition to erecting even large circles of mammoth stones, they buried their leaders in burial mounds lined with boulders and used a rudimentary form of a burial chamber in the tombs. Stonehenge was eventually abandoned about 1000 B.C., as part of another change that occurred during the last Bronze Age; the preference for cremation over burials for the dead became popular at that time. (Adapted from Janson, H. W. and Anthony F. *A Basic History of Art, 6th ed.* Upper Saddle River, N.J: Prentice Hall. 2003. 44–45)

6. "These immense stones were evidently dragged from Marlborough Downs, some twenty miles away—a feat as awesome as raising them, but it is a far from clear whether the inner bluestone circle and horseshoe, which date from several hundred years later (2480-1940 B.C.), were deposited by glaciers or carried by carts and rafts from the Preseli mountains in Wales some 200 miles to the west." (lines 9–14)

The above sentence is a statement of

a. fact.
b. opinion.

7. What is the overall tone of this passage?

a. praiseworthy
b. encouraging
c. informative
d. sentimental

8. A conclusion that can be drawn from this passage is that

a. the modifications in Stonehenge reflect the changes in the culture of the time.
b. until recently it was widely believed that Stonehenge was originally built to be lined up with the moonrises.
c. the desire for burials led to the desertion of Stonehenge.
d. people must have found a way to transport the stones from the inner bluestone circle and horseshoe.

Passage Three

Although Joan of Arc (Jeanne d'Arc) lived in the fifteenth century, she is essentially a figure of the late Middle Ages. She was born to a peasant family in the French village of Domremy during the Hundred Years War. As an illiterate girl of twelve, she heard voices from God instructing her to remain a virgin and rescue France from the English. This meant defending Charles VII's claim to the French throne. When she was seventeen, Joan persuaded a neighboring lord to present her to the king. At first, the king doubted that her voices were really sent by God, but his cause seemed doomed, so he was willing to try anything and agreed to equip her with armor and weapons. She rode into battle with the French troops at Orleans, giving them a new sense of national pride and inspiring them to victory. (Adams, Schneider Adams, *Exploring the Humanities: Creativity and Culture in the West*, Upper Saddle River, NJ: Prentice Hall, 2006. p. 302)

9. What is the overall tone of this passage?

    a. inspiring
    b. critical
    c. offensive
    d. reflective

10. A conclusion that can be drawn from this passage is that

    a. because Joan of Arc heard voices, the king of France thought she might be delusional.
    b. although illiterate, Joan of Arc implemented strategies on the battlefield that led France to victory over England.
    c. even though Joan of Arc was born into a peasant family, she learned to be very persuasive.
    d. although she was born into a peasant family, Joan of Arc was able to instill a new sense of pride in her countrymen and led them to an inspiring victory over England.

Read the statements below and determine the author's purpose by labeling them as entertaining, informative, or persuasive. Place an E in front of entertaining statements, an I before informative statements, and a P before persuasive statements.

_____1. Fireworks originated earlier than flame tests.

_____2. People with an incurable disease should be allowed to forego treatment that might prolong their lives.

_____3. One of the most famous of the cromlechs, a monumental stone structure made of huge blocks of boulders used singly or in groups, that was used for religious rites is Stonehenge in Southern England.

_____4. DNA fingerprinting can be used to establish parentage, convict a criminal, exonerate the innocent, and identify the dead.

_____5. Humor is produced by the social construction of reality; specifically, it arises as people create and contrast two different realities.

Answer Key Test 1

1. c
2. c
3. b
4. d
5. d
6. a
7. b
8. a
9. d
10. a

Author's Purpose

1. I
2. I
3. P
4. E
5. P

Answer Key Test 2

1. c
2. c
3. a
4. a
5. a
6. b
7. c
8. a
9. a
10. d

Author's Purpose

1. I
2. P
3. I
4. I
5. I

Chapter Ten: Evaluating Arguments

Summary

Sometimes in the midst of an argument, it becomes apparent to one or both of the people involved in the disagreement that they have lost sight of the point or reason for the argument. It is common to get so emotionally involved in an argument that you find yourself confused on the original issue or point you were trying to make. Because emotion often gets in the middle of any disagreement and can cloud judgment, developing good reasoning or analytical skills is extremely valuable. These skills require us to look at our own way of thinking and how we present our ideas.

Understanding argument means knowing when someone is trying to persuade you to believe something by the way they present promotions. Promotions usually make appeals to the reader's emotions, desires, or needs. Arguments appeal to the reader's intellect. Critical thinkers analyze persuasive text to separate promotions from arguments and locate the parts of an argument in essays and articles. Arguments have three main parts: the issue, the claim, and the reasons. The predict and verify approach, or PDQ3R, is a useful method for identifying these parts in argumentative essays and articles. This approach requires the reader to first look for or predict what the issue and claim are as they preread and divide. The reader must then question and read to verify his or her predictions and find the reasons. As they monitor and review the material in the text, readers need to pay particular attention to the author's reasons. Listing the reasons can help them judge how well the author is covering the issue and the claim. This list can also help readers determine their own opinions on the issue.

In academic and professional settings people are expected to engage in conversations that may be argumentative by presenting reasons to support their opinions. If we want others to understand our logic or reasoning, we must make an effort to be clear and concise when making a point that may be considered argumentative. If you want others to see your point of view, stating your point clearly and having supporting evidence to back it up will be two determining factors in persuading others that your argument is logical. Being able to think through such a process, identify important issues, look for answers, evaluate the evidence, and justify your position is known as critical thinking.

Critical thinking is an intellectual rather than an emotional approach that is used to analyze and evaluate issues, events, and problems. Critical thinking skills are important in reading, especially when it comes to evaluating an author's use of reasoning. Critical thinkers are skeptical. They question what they hear and read, and they question claims that are presented without support of proof. However, critical thinkers are also fair-minded and open to new ideas and opinions even when they do not agree with them.

To evaluate reasoning, you must be able to recognize the difference between various kinds of support for an argument including reliability and logic. Reliability, or trustworthiness, is determined by reviewing the author's credentials, purpose, and use of support. To judge the logic or reasoning behind statements made by an author, critical thinkers examine the strengths in an argument, but they also look for weaknesses, including bias and logical fallacies. Being able to determine if an author's rationale is valid, a reader needs to understand bias, a one-sided view. Bias occurs when an author omits important information, makes sweeping generalizations about a subject, or uses slated language to try and influence reader's opinions.

Reading with a critical eye also requires an understanding of how authors sometimes use logical fallacies, or mistakes in reasoning, to mislead readers. Logical fallacies come from faulty assumptions. Seven common fallacies discussed in this chapter are bandwagon, slippery slope, either-or-thinking, hasty generalization, questionable cause, non sequitur, and abstraction. Knowing how to assess biased viewpoint is the key to correctly interpreting what you are reading and determining whether the author's point is justified. When evaluating what they read, critical thinkers support their judgments with proof from the text.

Teaching Tips:

- When reading argument, encourage students to search for information that opposes the author's position as well as information that supports it. This will enable students to gain a more objective view of the issue.

- Explain to students that many argumentative statements involve the use of the word **should**. The word **should** express opinion and bias and is something that readers want to be careful of when evaluating reasoning. A sound argument presents facts that can be supported by evidence.

- Tie understanding argument to the importance of knowing the difference between fact and opinion. Explain that authors who present an argument using a lot opinion and bias are not giving readers a balanced or objective view of the issue. Readers need the facts so they can make informed decisions, but often authors give them a mix of fact and opinion. That is why understanding the difference between what is fact and what is opinion is so important.

The following key terms can help students better understand what is involved in evaluating the author's reasoning in an argument.

1. **Adequate or Inadequate Support** – Is there enough information available to draw a rational and logical conclusion about the issue?

2. **Relevant or Irrelevant Support** – Is the information being presented as support for an argument actually related to the point being argued? Don't be misled by information that really has nothing to do with the issue being discussed.

3. **Objective support** – Is the information being offered as support for the argument being presented without bias or prejudice. In other words, is the reader being given both sides of the issue so they can make an informed decision?

4. **Emotional Support** – Is the information being offered as support for the argument being presented with a strong generalized feeling?

   Example: "Abortion is murder, and under no circumstance should any woman be allowed to have an abortion."

   Abortion is both a controversial and emotional issue. While people are certainly entitled to their opinions, you cannot effectively evaluate an issue based on emotion. Many other factors have to be examined when making decisions that can affect a lot of people.

5. **Valid or Invalid Points** – Is the information for the argument sound or well-grounded on principals or evidence. In other words, has the author gathered enough convincing research that makes use of the facts to prove his point?

Suggested Activities:

- Set up structured controversy. Present a statement for argument. Divide the class into three groups. Have one of the groups come up with four factual support points in favor of the argument. Have another group come up with four factual support points against the argument. Have the third group serve as panel of judges. Next, ask each group charged with developing support points for the argument to select a person to present its points. Set up a circle of chairs. Have each student sit in a circle with the exception of the two presenters and the panel of judges. Take two chairs and place them in the center of the circle so the presenters are facing one another. Seat the panel of judges nearby so they can hear the points and observe the presenters. Explain to the presenters and the rest of the class that support points must be clearly stated and above all no sarcastic remarks will be permitted. Flip a coin to see which presenter will begin. Then, have the first presenter make one point statement. Stress that the presenter must be allowed to make his or her point without being interrupted. After the first presenter finishes making a point, have the second presenter respond with one point. Stress again that each presenter must be allowed to make his or her point without being interrupted. Have the presenters do this until they exhausted all the support points for each side of the argument. Have the panel of judges assess each of the presenter's points and identify both the strengths and weaknesses of the points. Have the judges decide which presenter delivered the most convincing support points.

- Provide students with two editorials from different newspapers or magazines on the same topic. Next, have students write the main idea and evidence for each article. Then, have the students determine if the evidence is based in fact or opinion. Ask students to evaluate the evidence and determine what was not included in the articles that they think should have been included. Finally, have them determine which view they feel presents the best argument.

- Put students in groups and have them collaborate on a topic for an editorial or an editorial cartoon. Then have the students compile information for the editorial or draw an editorial cartoon.

- Read the following newspaper editorial that appeared in the Florida Times Union on December 14, 2003. Determine if the author has given you enough information to make an informed decision. Look to see if the author uses emotionally loaded words. Determine if the author is presenting an objective viewpoint or a bias view of the subject.

Editorial

Rebuilding Iraq will be a job for nations that helped establish the need to rebuild, President Bush has declared, appropriately.

France, Germany and Russia, which sat on their thumbs while the United States and its allies liberated the 25 million oppressed citizens of Iraq, now want to profit by getting major contracts to rebuild the infrastructure.

Bush said the $18.6 billion in contracts will go to the members of the U.S.-led coalition.

Other nations are free to help. For example, they hold a good part of the $125 billion in debt Iraq owes. By forgiving or restructuring that debt, they can aid immensely—and it won't cost them a single life.

Should they balk, or try to use the debt issue as a bargaining chip to get contracts, they may find that the Iraqi people will choose simply to ignore the debt, which is more properly owed by Saddam Hussein than them.

Liberals say Bush may be violating "international law." As everyone but a few liberal justices on the Supreme Court realizes, the law in the United States is the U.S. Constitution.

Liberals also say the United States needs more international goodwill and that this decision does not generate much.

That's true. But the nation needs friends through thick and thin, not slackers who only show up on payday.

Britain, as always, has been there. So have more than 30 other nations.

The anti-American contingent has one point: limiting competition may result in slightly higher costs.

U.S. taxpayers are going to pay for the reconstruction. Ask them whether they want to pay a little more or let French companies profit now, after France did everything it could to thwart the liberation of Iraq.

Now that you have read the editorial, ask yourself the following questions:

1. Is the author's claim in line one that rebuilding Iraq should be a job for nations that helped establish the need to rebuild adequately supported by fact or inadequately supported because of a lack of factual evidence? Explain your answer.

2. Which of the following statements offer the best support for the author's claim that the nation needs friends through thick and thin, not slackers who only show up on payday? (lines 19–20)

   a. France, Germany and Russia, which sat on their thumbs while the United States and its allies liberated the 25 million oppressed citizens of Iraq, now want to profit by getting major contracts to rebuild the infrastructure.
   b. Liberals say Bush may be violating "international law." As everyone but a few liberal justices on the Supreme Court realizes, the law in the United States is the U.S. Constitution.
   c. U.S. taxpayers are going to pay for the reconstruction.
   d. Other nations are free to help. For example, they hold a good part of the $125 billion in debt Iraq owes.

3. What, if any, emotionally loaded words does the author use in the editorial?

4. Is the author is presenting an objective viewpoint or a biased view of the subject? Find and list support for your answer.

   Answers will vary, but some comments might include the following statements:

   1. Yes. The editorial explains that the coalition did the work of liberating Iraq and thus deserves to get the work of rebuilding.
   2. D.
   3. "France, Germany and Russia ... sat on their thumbs..."
   4. Answers will vary
   5. A biased view of the subject. An objective viewpoint devoid of opinion would not be an editorial, which is by definition the newspaper's opinion of an issue.

Evaluating Arguments Test 1

Passage 1

Global warming is under way, and the warming is making it hard for the polar bears around Churchill, Manitoba, to find enough to eat. Churchill lies on the southwest shore of Hudson's Bay and is a port for oceangoing vessels that carry grain produced on the Canadian Prairies to foreign destinations. The bay is frozen much of the year, so the port is only open for a brief period from midsummer to autumn. While the ice is a barrier to shipping, it is essential for the polar bears who inhabit the region. They feed largely on seal pups, which they catch in snow lairs that the seal create over breathing holes in the sea ice. When the bay is ice-free, the seals spend most of their time in the water, safe from the bears. The summer is thus the hungry season for the bears.

Over the last few decades, temperatures in central and northern Canada have been gradually rising. It is expected that global warming will be felt most strongly in high latitudes, and there is considerable evidence that these effects are occurring now in Churchill. Today the ice melts in Hudson Bay about three weeks earlier in the summer than it did 25 years ago, and it is freezing later in the fall. That means that the hungry season for the bears is lasting several weeks longer, and the bears are having a harder time making it through the summer. It is expected that the warming will ultimately force the bears to migrate northward, and the tundra vegetation around Churchill will be replaced with species normally found much farther south. (Bergman, Edward F. and Renwick, William H., Introduction to Geography People, Places, and Environment, 2nd ed. Upper Saddle River, NJ: Prentice Hall, 2003. 130)

1. The author's claim that global warming is making it hard for polar bears around Churchill, Manitoba, to find enough to eat (lines 1–2) is

    a.   adequately supported by personal experience and strongly held opinion.
    b.   inadequately supported because of the lack of factual evidence.

2. Which statement offers the best support for the author's claim that hungry season for the bears is lasting several weeks longer, and the bears are having a harder time making it through the summer? (lines 14–16)

    a.   The summer is thus the hungry season for the bears.
    b.   Today the ice melts in Hudson Bay about three weeks earlier in the summer than it did 25 years ago, and it is freezing later in the fall.
    c.   It is expected that the warming will ultimately force the bears to migrate northward, and the tundra vegetation around Churchill will be replaced with species normally found much farther south.
    d.   It is expected that global warming will be felt most strongly in high latitudes, and there is considerable evidence that these effects are occurring now in Churchill.

Passage 2

Computer culture—in the form of electronic mail, word processing, the World Wide Web, "cyberpunk," arcade-style games, chat rooms, hypertext, digital multimedia, and on and on—is no longer merely an emerging phenomenon; it has become a driving force in contemporary America and the world. In fact, computers have become so much a part of our lives that the social conventions surrounding computers have taken on the importance of Biblical commandments. Furthermore, the culture surrounding computers evolves with such rapidity that many people find themselves confused, awash in a white-noise sea of nagging questions; what is the meaning of those weird terms—gigabytes and baud rates and MOOs and flaming—that tech-nerds use; is nonlinear writing as modeled by the World Wide Web and other hypertext-formatted documents, really going to replace traditional expository writing, with its linear logical, structure; will the average individual need to be fully computer literate to survive and even prosper in the economy of the next millennium; how will the computer redefine people's notions of work, leisure time, and social interaction; how will the aesthetic worlds of music and visual art be influenced by the continuing use of computer technology; and will "virtual reality"—the real-time, interactive, computerized simulation of sensory experiences—become a practical reality in succeeding decades? (Information in this passage has been adapted from Petracca, Michael and Sorapure, Madeleine, Common Culture: Reading and Writing About American Popular Culture, 3rd ed. Upper Saddle River, NJ: Prentice Hall, 2001. 333)

3. The authors claim that the computer culture has become a driving force in contemporary America and the world is

   a. adequately supported by personal experience and strongly held opinion.
   b. inadequately supported because of the lack of factual evidence.

4. Which statement offers the best support for the author's claim that the computer culture is no longer merely an emerging phenomenon?

   a. It has become a driving force in contemporary America and the world.
   b. Computers have become so much a part of our lives that the social conventions surrounding computers have taken on the importance of Biblical commandments.
   c. The culture surrounding computers evolves with such rapidity that many people find themselves confused, awash in a white-noise sea of nagging questions.
   d. Will the average individual need to be fully computer literate to survive and even prosper in the economy of the next millennium?

Passage 3

Arachnids have a dreadful reputation in Florida, but there are only two types of spiders that are venomous to humans compared to the numerous types of spiders that regularly inhabit this state. The widow spider is the only venomous spider that is native to this state; the other type of poisonous spider, the recluse spider, was introduced to Florida from other places such as Chile and the Mediterranean. Both types of toxic spiders prefer to dwell under objects such as logs, rocks, furniture, and buildings where they will remain hidden from their predators and prey.

There are four categories of widow spiders that all share some physical and behavioral characteristics. Widow spiders' bodies are approximately one-quarter to one-half inch long, with a shiny, rounded abdomen on which there is a red hourglass shape or reddish-orange shapes located on the underside. Some have black legs while others have reddish-brown legs, whitish legs, or banded legs. These spiders often build irregular-produced tent-like webs that have a denser cone shaped region in the center or at a corner in which they conceal themselves; these webs are most frequently located near the ground on the underside of objects, although they also situate their habitats in other vicinities.

Widow spiders are typically somewhat reserved spiders that generally attack only when someone reaching into a confined space where the spider is secreted ensnares them against the human skin, or by donning clothing in which the spider is concealed. Their bites may trigger intense discomfort, headache, nausea, cramping, breathing difficulties, hypertension, and rigidity of muscles, but there are two types of injections which relieve the symptoms, antivenin or calcium glucose. Most victims are only slightly affected with influenza symptoms, and unless they are very young, are elderly, or possess additional physical conditions, the symptoms usually disappear in three to five days. Recluse spiders have one-quarter to one-half inch sized bodies that vary in color from tan to dark brown with a dark violin shaped design on the front half of their head, but it is easier to recognize them by their eyes because they have three pairs of eyes instead of the customary eight pairs that most spiders possess.

Recluse spiders construct a web, but they often vacate their web to search for or pursue prey. Resembling the widow spiders, they typically only puncture humans when they are trapped adjacent to a victim's skin. Recluse bites may have very dissimilar symptoms in different victims; some have obvious inflammation, swelling, and reddish blisters, while others have no noticeable symptoms. If the wound is to become necrotic (tissue destroying), it will usually become purple in color within twelve to twenty-four hours, and then it will turn darker as the tissue dies; eventually a cavity in the skin will remain. There is no antivenin at the present time, but treatment within twenty-four hours with corticosteroids does alleviate some of the symptoms.

With any spider bite, it is imperative to cleanse the wound and to capture or preserve the spider that bit the victim, even if it is in pieces, because this will make it possible for the physician to care for to the wound with the appropriate measures.

5. The author's claim that "Most victims are only slightly affected with influenza symptoms, and unless they are very young, are elderly, or possess additional physical conditions, the symptoms usually disappear in three to five days" is

   a. adequately supported by examples.
   b. inadequately supported because of lack of evidence.

6. In this passage, the author expresses a biased attitude for

   a. keeping your hands way from secluded places under objects.
   b. disliking spiders that can make you ill or even kill you.
   c. taking antivenin for all spider bites.
   d. cleaning spider wounds.

Passage 4

As an interesting exercise, carry a trash bag around for a single day and collect everything you throw away. Most people are surprised to find that the average person in the United States discards almost 5 pounds of paper, metal, plastic, and other materials daily (over a lifetime, that's about 50 tons). For the country as a whole, this amounts to about 1 billion pounds of solid waste each and every day.

As a rich nation containing people who value convenience, the United States has become a *disposable society*. We consume more products than virtually any other nation on Earth, and much of them have throwaway packaging. The most familiar case is fast food, served with cardboard, plastic, and styrofoam containers that we throw away within minutes. However, countless other products—from film to fishhooks—are elaborately packaged to make the product more attractive to the customer and discourage tampering and theft.

Consider, too, that manufacturers market soft drinks, beer, and fruit juices in aluminum cans, glass, jars, and plastic containers, which not only consume finite resources but also generate mountains of solid waste. Then there are countless items intentionally designed to be disposable: pens, razors, flashlights, batteries, even cameras. Other goods, from light bulbs to automobiles, are designed to have limited useful life and then become unwanted junk. As Paul H. Connett, author of "The Disposable Society," points out, even the words we use to describe what we throw away "waste," "litter," "trash," "refuse," "garbage," "rubbish"—show how little we value what we cannot immediately use.

Living in a rich society, the average person in the United States consumes 50 times more steel, 170 times more newspaper, 250 times more gasoline, and 300 times more plastic each year than the typical person in India. This high level of consumption means that we in the United States not only use a disproportionate share of the planet's natural resources but also generate most of the world's refuse.

We like to say that we "throw things away." But 80 percent of our solid waste is not burned or recycled and never "goes away." Rather, it ends up in landfills, which are, literally, filling up. Materials in landfills also can pollute groundwater. Although in most places laws now regulate what can be discarded in a landfill, the Environmental Protection agency has identified 30,000 dump sites across the United States containing hazardous materials that are polluting water both above and below the ground. In addition, what goes into landfills all too often stays there, sometimes for centuries. Tens of millions of tires, diapers, and other items that we bury in landfills each year do not decompose and will be an unwelcome legacy for future generations.

Environmentalists argue that we should address the problem of solid waste by doing what many of our ancestors did: Turn "waste" into a resource. One way to do this is through recycling, reusing resources we would otherwise discard. Recycling is an accepted practice in Japan and many other nations, and it is becoming more common in the United States, where we now reuse about 30 percent of waste materials. The share is increasing as laws mandate reuse of certain materials such as glass bottles and aluminum cans. In addition, because our nation has a market-based economy, recycling is bound to increase as it becomes more profitable. (Marconis, John J., Society The Basics. 7th ed. Upper Saddle River, NJ: Prentice Hall, 2004. 424–425)

7. In this passage, the author expresses a biased attitude against

   a. recycling cans and bottles.
   b. land fills.
   c. extraneous packaging.
   d. film and fishhooks.

8. The author's claim that "This high level of consumption means that we in the United States not only use a disproportionate share of the planet's natural resources but also generate most of the world's refuse." (lines 23–25) is

   a. adequately supported by examples.
   b. inadequately supported because of lack of evidence.

Passage 5

The average student spends a lot of time thinking about his or her body and ways to make it more attractive. While most people realize that there are a wide range of body types and sizes, attractiveness tends to be more narrowly defined by the images of men and women we see in the popular media; and nearly all media images equate attractiveness and desirability with a limited range of body types.

For men, the image of a tall, broad-shouldered, muscular man with so little body fat that every muscle is visible is portrayed as most desirable.

The standards for female beauty are unforgiving also. Images of female beauty are almost exclusively women with small hips; long, thin limbs; large breasts; and no body fat.

This is virtually the only image of female beauty seen in fashion magazines, on billboards, on television, and in the movies.

Into this milieu steps the average college students—worried about appearance, trying to find time to study, exercise, and socialize and now making all his or her own decisions about food, often on a limited budget.

Making choices that are good for long-term health is not easy. The typical dining-center meal-plan choices, often greasy and fat-laden, are available in unlimited portions. The difficulty of making healthful choices is compounded by the presence of campus snack shops, vending machines, and conveniently located fast-food restaurants that offer time-pressed students easily accessible, inexpensive foods containing little nutrition. Coupling tremendous pressure to be thin with a glut of readily available unhealthful foods can lead to the establishment of unhealthful eating habits that persist far beyond college life. In many cases, these conflicting pressures can lead students to develop eating habits that result in a lifelong battle with obesity or starvation, along with their associated health risks. (Material in this passage was adapted from Belk, Colleen and Virginia Borden. *Biology Science for Life. 1ˢᵗ ed.* Upper Saddle River, NJ: Prentice Hall, 2004. 23)

9. In this passage, the author expresses a biased attitude against

    a. unattractive people.
    b. media images of beauty.
    c. college students.
    d. healthy food.

10. The author's claim that "making choices that are good for long-term health is not easy" is

    a. adequately supported by examples.
    b. inadequately supported because of lack of evidence.

Fill in the missing information for the questions below

1. Persuasion is designed to convince readers by presenting _____ or _____.

2. Promotions usually make appeals to the reader's _____, _____, or _____.

3. Arguments appeal to the reader's _____.

4. Critical thinkers analyze persuasive text to separate _____ from _____.

5. Because emotion often gets in the middle of any disagreement and can cloud judgment, developing

_____ _____ or _____ _____ is extremely valuable.

Evaluating Arguments Test 2

_____ 1. argue
_____ 2. bias
_____ 3. claim
_____ 4. critical thinking
_____ 5. fair-minded

_____ 6. logical fallacies

_____ 7. promotions
_____ 8. reasons

_____ 9. reliability
_____ 10. skepticism

a. open to new ideas and opinions
b. an author's position or opinion
c. trustworthiness
d. a one-sided presentation
e. maintaining doubt when claims are presented without support or proof
f. explanations given by the author to support his or her claim
g. appeal to a reader's emotions, desires, or needs
h. reasons that support of a particular opinion or point of view
i. mistakes in reasoning
j. the ability to objectively examine and evaluate events, issues, and problems

Label the following phrases with a "T" if it is a topic and an "I" if it is an issue

_____ a. the right to die with dignity

_____ b. abortion

_____ c. war

_____ d. poverty in the United States

_____ e. the legalization of abortion

Answer Key Test 1

Passage 1
1. a
2. b

Passage 2
3. a
4. a

Passage 3
5. b
6. d

Passage 4
7. c
8. a

Passage 5

9. b
10. a

Missing information

1. promotions; arguments
2. emotions, desires, or needs
3. intellect
4. promotions; arguments
5. good reasoning; analytical skills

Answer Key Test 2

Matching

1. h
2. d
3. b
4. j
5. a
6. i
7. g
8. f
9. c
10. e

Topic or Issue Phrases

1. I
2. T
3. T
4. I
5. I

Diagnostic Test 1

1. Joyce can be OBSTINATE sometimes; once she has made a plan, she will never change it.
   - a. open-minded
   - b. considerate
   - c. stubborn
   - d. thoughtful

2. We were AGHAST when we learned that Sheila and Joe were splitting up.
   - a. shocked
   - b. happy
   - c. flamboyant
   - d. angry

3. I've been filled with a sense of FOREBODING since the computer screen flickered earlier; just know our system is going to crash today.
   - a. apprehension
   - b. happiness
   - c. sadness
   - d. strain

4. I know Doug doesn't smoke, but there is no need for him to be SANCTIMONIOUS about it; it doesn't make him a better person.
   - a. self-righteous
   - b. bitter
   - c. humble
   - d. angry

5. Mother Teresa's PHILANTHROPIC work with the poor made her a household name.
   - a. poor
   - b. charitable
   - c. difficult
   - d. worthless

6. Many online auction services have a CAVEAT EMPTOR policy; they don't guarantee anything you buy from them.
   - a. warranty
   - b. as is
   - c. money back
   - d. coupon

7. Tom is an ARDENT hunter; he takes off work nearly a month every year for deer season.
   - a. careless
   - b. indifferent
   - c. dedicated
   - d. harsh

8. The fight had MARRED his face badly. His eyes were swollen, his nose was broken, and his cheeks were black and blue.
   - a. disfigured
   - b. helped
   - c. softened
   - d. weakened

9. Charles serves as the NUCLEUS of our group; if he did not function as the mid-point around which all our friends gather, we would drift apart.

   a. leader   c. center
   b. power   d. coordinator

10. My math teachers spent many hours trying to KINDLE in me an interest in algebra.

    a. interest   c. eliminate
    b. create   d. multiply

Stated Main Idea

Instructions: Write the number of the main idea sentence in the blank below each paragraph.

11.   1In the last part of the Paleozoic Era, erosion so lowered the level of great areas of the continents that numerous large swamps formed. 2The partly decayed swamp vegetation slowly accumulated on the swamp bottom and was gradually converted to peat. 3Centuries later, after the peat was buried and compressed beneath sediments, it slowly changed into coal. 4These great deposits of Paleozoic coal make up one of the largest concentrations of carbon on earth and certainly one of the greatest sources of energy available today. 5Coal and shale beds formed during the Pennsylvania Period are shown on page 440. (Bisque & Heller, *Investigating the Earth*)

       Main Idea _____

12.   1But fundamentalism was hardly destroyed, and antirevolutionists continued their campaign. 2New organizations, such as the Bryan Bible League, lobbied for state laws and an antievolution amendment to the constitution. 3Three more states forbade teaching evolution, but by 1929 the movement had faltered. 4Even so, fundamentalism retained religious influence and would again challenge science and modernism in American life. (Goldfield et al., *The American Journey*)

       Main Idea _____

13.   1Muhammad, the prophet of Islam, was born about 570 in Mecca, in west-central Arabia. 2His family traced their ancestry to Ishmael, a son of the Hebrew patriarch Abraham. 3One night in 610 CE, since called by Muslims "The Night of Power and Excellence," Muhammad, at that time named al-Amin (the Trusted One), sought solitude in a cave on Mount Hira, a few miles north of Mecca. 4There the angel Gabriel is believed to have appeared to him and commanded him to recite revelations from God. 5At that moment, al-Amin became Muhammad, the Messenger of God. (Stokstad, *Art: A Brief History*)

       Main Idea _____

14.   1Since the courts so clearly favored employers, labor turned to Congress to redress the proemployer bias in labor policy. 2Early in this century, Congress passed a series of acts designed to provide that redress, but they were either declared unconstitutional or interpreted by the Supreme Court as still permitting the courts to determine whether particular labor activities were "lawful," "legitimate," and "peaceful." 3It was not until 1932 and the passage of the **Norris-La Guardia Act** that the general labor movement achieved a notable victory in its struggle with management. (Watson, *Promise and Performance of American Democracy*)

Main Idea _____

15.   1Another kind of land subsidence, the occurrence of a sinkhole, may be sudden and dramatic. 2A sinkhole results when an underground cavern, drained of its supporting groundwater, suddenly collapses. 3Sinkholes may be at least 300 feet across and as much as 150 feet deep. 4Formation of sinkholes is particularly severe in the southeastern United States, where groundwater has leached numerous passageways and caverns through ancient beds of underlying limestone. 5An estimated 4000 sinkholes have occurred in Alabama alone, some of which have "consumed" buildings, livestock, and sections of highways. (Nebel & Wright, *Environmental Science*)

Main Idea _____

Implied Main Idea

Instructions: Read each paragraph below, then read the three sentences underneath the paragraph. Indicate which sentence best reflects the main idea of the paragraph.

16.   Sarah Orne Jewett, in *Country of the Pointed Firs*, rises above social conventions. Her characters are a realistic blend of traditional masculine and feminine traits. The characters, both male and female, who live in Dunnet Landing do not operate within the constraints of stereotypical conventions. In this way she achieves realism. Jewett's characters are a literary realization of the fact that stereotypes are simply convenient, or sometimes inconvenient, social constructs, and not irrefutable facts of nature.

   a. Sarah Orne Jewett is an unconventional writer because of her disregard of stereotypes.
   b. Jewett's disregard of stereotypes lends her work an air of realism.
   c. Jewett's characters, both male and female, are realistic in nature.

17. Jewett, in the blending of masculine and feminine attributes in her characters, masterfully portrays a truth that many writers of her period would overlook. The truth is that women are not weak, simpering, dependent creatures incapable of sustained productive endeavor. Men are not always strong, independent providers and protectors. People of either gender are multi-faceted, difficult to conclusively categorize, and usually possess traits common to either stereotype.

   a. Jewett realizes that women are not weak, simpering creatures.
   b. Jewett's strength lies in realizing that men are not always strong and independent.
   c. Jewett's strength lies in her rejection of stereotypes of both sexes.

18. In *A Doll's House*, Torvald's naturalization of stereotypical roles has cost him his marriage; it has damaged his self respect; it once nearly cost him his health—he is a victim of an unrealistic illusion of power and invulnerability. But one more thing must be said regarding Torvald's character. While there is reason for sympathy for Torvald, we must remember that there is a way out of the cycle of illusion and victimization. Nora has found the means and the courage to escape her role and the demands of a marriage founded on illusion. Torvald has not the courage to walk out of his current life, and though there is hope that he will come to see himself and Nora more clearly, if he does not see, it will be because he has closed his eyes.

   a. We should have sympathy for Torvald because of the tragedies that have befallen him.
   b. Nora was the true victim of their marriage of illusion.
   c. The tragedies in Torvald's life are largely of his own making.

19. In the staging of his plays, Bertolt Brecht made certain that the machinery and lights were clearly visible to the audience. The audience is supposed to remember that it is watching a play, and this alienation makes it easier to see a structured performance rather than a naturally progressive "slice of life" in the play. Despite our sympathy for Mother Courage's losses and our indignation at the injustices of war, we are able to step back to see the larger framework of these events. Through this mechanism, Brecht hoped that we would be taught to step back and examine the larger framework of our world.

   a. Bertolt Brecht wanted his audiences to be drawn into his plays and to forget the larger world outside.
   b. Brecht wanted his audiences to see his plays as plays rather than being drawn into the dramatic world.
   c. Brecht made certain that the audience could see the machinery of the theater during his plays.

20. The hall is full of old men "pathetic in their dissipation" and of boys with "mouths of sin." These men and boys look at Maggie through clouds of smoke reminiscent of the sulphurous fumes of Hell. The submissive orchestra could be a picture of lost souls under the control of a "frowsy" fiend. The singer wears a "flaming" scarlet dress, and the noise drifting through the smoke causes Maggie to dream of her days in Rum Alley—another kind of Hell. The infernal atmosphere of this dance hall mirrors well the atmosphere of this whole work.

    a. The dance hall described is full of evil men and lost souls.
    b. The dance hall is described in terms meant to invoke an image of Hell.
    c. Maggie does not like being here, and dreams of her days in Rum Alley.

Instructions: Read the passage, paying close attention to main ideas, support, and coherence. Answer the questions which follow.

1The Greeks were able to measure the angle of the noon sun and to observe the arc of the sun's path across the sky. 2They had also found the length of daylight and darkness for the longest and shortest days of the year at various places on earth. 3From these observations, latitudinal zones called *climata* were established that had approximately the same period of sunlight on any given day of the year. 4Greek astronomers and philosophers were very interested in the average length of days. 5Eventually the word *climata* signified the temperature conditions in these zones also.

1In thinking about the size and shape of the world and using the climatic data available to them, the Greek philosophers speculated that climatic zones similar to those they had observed in the Northern Hemisphere existed in the Southern Hemisphere. 2Some of them even thought that a continent must exist south of the equator. 3They called this continent Atlantis. 4Out of these speculations came a division of the earth into five major climatic zones. 5The zones are identified in Figure 11–4. (Bisque & Heller, *Investigating the Earth*)

21. Which of the following sentences best states the controlling idea of this passage? _____

    a. Out of the speculations of the Greeks came the division into five major climatic zones.
    b. The Greeks discovered a continent south of the equator.
    c. Greek philosophers and astronomers invented climatic zones.
    d. Climata signifies the temperature and hours of sunlight of a given place.

22. What is the number of the main idea sentence of the first paragraph? _____

23. What is the number of the main idea sentence of the second paragraph? _____

24. What is the number of the sentence which does not belong in the first paragraph? _____

25. What is the number of the sentence which does not belong in the second paragraph? _____

1It is through the action of water, wind, and ice in response to gravity that erosion occurs. 2These agents relentlessly wear down the land and transport loose material from the land to the sea. 3The journey for most mineral and rock particles is long and winding. 4A particle might come to rest in a given place for thousands of years before it is picked up again and moved along. 5This process may be repeated many times before material loosened from a mountain cliff eventually reaches the sea. 6Some of this material may reach incredible depths.

1Soil may be considered as a temporary depository of weathered material. 2Soil is necessary for agriculture. 3Soil may form on solid rock or it may be formed on sediments that are deposited on their way to the sea. 4The amount of soil now on the land is the difference between the amount of soil produced by weathering and the amount of soil that has been removed by erosion. 5Why are thin, rocky soils commonly found in mountainous regions? (Bisque & Heller, *Investigating the Earth*)

26. What is the number of the main idea sentence in the first paragraph? _____

27. What is the number of the main idea sentence in the second paragraph? _____

28. What is the number of the sentence which does not belong in the first paragraph? _____

29. What is the number of the sentence which does not belong in the second paragraph? _____

30. Why are thin, rocky soils commonly found in mountainous regions? _____

    a. The wind often blows thin soils back up onto mountains.
    b. Erosion on mountains is very slow, and does not break up the rocks.
    c. The erosion process does not allow deep soil buildup on mountainsides.
    d. Soil does not form on solid rock.

Instructions: Read the following paragraphs. Answer the questions following each one.

    Gun control laws simply don't work. Research has shown that violent crime rates go up in states hat introduce stricter gun control legislation. Look at New York City and Washington, D.C.; they have the toughest gun laws in the country, and they still have two of the highest violent crime rates as well. We need to find another way to curb gun violence.

31. The author's tone is _____.

    a. admiring   c. neutral
    b. begrudging   d. persuasive

32. The author is strongly biased against _____.

    a. New York City   c. gun control laws
    b. not apparent   d. Washington, D.C. laws.

Teenagers today don't realize how easy their lives are. They get everything handed to them on a silver platter, and they complain when asked to do chores or anything else that takes them away from their video games and CD collections. When I was a boy, we didn't even have indoor plumbing, much less electricity; now my grandson thinks going without TV for a couple of days is punishment.

33. The author's tone is: _____

    a. admiring   c. neutral
    b. contemptuous   d. persuasive

34. The author is strongly biased against: _____

    a. today's teens   c. video games
    b. not apparent   d. TV Reading Rate

Educators today face many tough challenges. They must educate their students, keep up with mountains of paperwork, be moral guides, and stay current in their own fields. And we expect them to do this on a salary that wouldn't feed a good-sized pet. We should be more appreciative of our teachers.

35. The author's tone is _____.

    a. admiring   c. neutral
    b. begrudging   d. indignant

36. The author is strongly biased against _____.

    a. principals   c. teachers
    b. not apparent   d. parents

Despite the harmful impacts intrinsic to cultivation, systems of crop rotations—a cash crop such as corn, with hay and clover (which fixes nitrogen as well as adding organic matter) in between—have proved sustainable. However, as food or economic demands cause the abandonment of rotations, degradation and erosion exceed regenerative processes, and the result is a gradual decline in soil quality, or desertification. This is the essence of overcultivation. (Nebel & Wright, *Environmental Science*)

37. The author's tone is _____.

    a. admiring   c. neutral
    b. cautionary   d. persuasive

38. The author is strongly biased against _____.

    a. cultivation   c. crop rotation
    b. not apparent   d. cash crops

    Smoking, like alcohol and other drugs, is considered to be a personal pollutant because it is a cultural hazard people expose themselves to on a voluntary basis. Unfortunately, recent trends show that people are likely to start smoking at a younger age. Lured by the image of smoking as "cool" or by peer pressure, youngsters are soon addicted to the nicotine in cigarettes, an addiction that is difficult to break. Smoking is, essentially, portable air pollution. (Nebel & Wright *Environmental Science*)

39. The author's tone is _____.

    a. admiring   c. neutral
    b. cautionary   d. critical

40. The author is strongly biased against _____.

    a. smoking   c. young smokers
    b. not apparent   d. recent trends

Instructions: Read the passage. When you are finished, answer the questions.

Showdown in the New West (Nebel & Wright, *Environmental Science*)

    In a scenario reminiscent of the Civil War, two western states have become the focus of a controversy over states' rights. On one side is the federal government, in the form of the Department of Energy, which is trying to solve the problem of what to do with nuclear wastes and thinks it has a reasonable solution. On the other side are politicians in the states designated as repository sites, who are responding to the voices of citizens of those states. At stake may be the whole future of nuclear energy in the United States.

    The Department of Energy has constructed a $1.5 billion Waste Isolation Pilot Plant (WIPP) in salt caves 2150 feet beneath the desert in southwestern New Mexico, 26 miles from the city of Carlsbad. The plant is on federal land and has passed all necessary safety reviews. It was ready to open for business in October 1991. "Business," in this case, was for the plant to become the repository for up to a million barrels of plutonium wastes from nuclear weapons plants and laboratories around the country, as well as the plutonium from dismantled nuclear warheads. (No commercial nuclear wastes will go there.) Eager to prove that nuclear wastes can be safely moved and placed in such a repository, the energy agency wants to bring a few thousand barrels to the New Mexico site in order to demonstrate the usefulness of the facility. The main objection to the New Mexico site is the prospect of accidents on the narrow roads in the area. There was talk of barricades in the streets to block the trucks if the Energy Department starts them rolling.

New Mexico sued the Department of Energy on the grounds that it was in violation of federal law prohibiting the opening of such a repository without congressional approval. The state of Texas and four environmental groups joined New Mexico in bringing suit. In October 1992, Congress gave approval to the department to begin testing the facility's ability to store the plutonium wastes—with one significant catch: the EPA was ordered to strengthen the radiation standards protecting the public from the stored wastes. After a lengthy review, the EPA gave the WIPP certification in 1998 to begin receiving radioactive materials from nuclear weapons facilities around the country, and the process is under way.

Opposition to long-term storage of nuclear wastes is perhaps even stronger in Nevada, which has the dubious distinction of being selected for the nation's only repository for *commercial* nuclear wastes, at Yucca Mountain. The site is a barren ridge in the desert about 100 miles northwest of Las Vegas. In 1989, the Nevada legislature passed a bill making it unlawful for any agent or agency to store high-level radioactive waste in the state. All sorts of surveys have been carried out to test the mood of Nevadans regarding long-term storage of wastes in their state. The results have been uniformly negative: three-fourths of Nevadans agreed that the state should continue to do all it can to prevent the establishment of the Yucca Mountain site. Clearly, ordinary Nevadans perceive the risks of such a site as enormous and unacceptable, in contrast to the opinions of scientists who have performed risk calculations for the site. In this case, however, the state's attempts to pose a legal blockade to the Department of Energy have failed; the Supreme Court has ruled that Nevada must process applications for permits to continue work on the site. In drafting the recent Nuclear Waste Policy Act of 1997 for establishing an interim storage facility at Yucca Mountain, Congress expressly preempted all state, local, or tribal laws that might pose an obstacle to implementing the bill. Thus, the state of Nevada is obliged to cooperate with the establishment of Yucca Mountain if it indeed does get either interim or final approval from Congress.

The dilemma is plain. Public and political support for any form of nuclear energy is at an all-time low, and people in these two western states are especially indignant at their states' becoming the repository of nuclear wastes from around the nation. Yet we need to do something with the legacy of nuclear energy other than to pass the problem along to the next generation. What do you think should be done?

Word Count: 725   Minutes: _____   Rate: _____

41. This passage is primarily about _____.

   a. New Mexico and Nevada fighting over nuclear energy
   b. the federal government and state governments fighting over nuclear waste disposal
   c. opposition to storage of nuclear wastes

42. Opposition to the storage facilities stems from _____.

   a. the Environmental Protection Agency
   b. Congress and the Department of Energy
   c. citizens of New Mexico and Nevada

43. T or F   New Mexico sued the Department of Energy.

44. T or F   Citizens of New Mexico blockaded streets to prevent the passage of trucks carrying nuclear waste.

45. New Mexico's storage facility will house _____.

    a. military nuclear waste
    b. commercial nuclear waste
    c. high-level radioactive waste

Instructions: After reading the paragraph below, label the following details as Main Idea (MI), Major Detail (MJ), or Minor Detail (MN).

In general, span of control and decentralization are often interrelated. For example, if lower-level managers are given *more* decision-making authority, their supervisors will thus have *less* work to do because some of the decisions they previously made will be transferred to their subordinates. By the same token, these managers may then be able to oversee and coordinate the work of more subordinates, resulting in an increased span of control. When the changes previously described were implemented at Toyota, senior managers saw their spans of control increase from between 5 and 7 to 10 and 12 employees each. (Ebert & Griffin, *Business Essentials*)

46. The spans of control at Toyota increased after making these changes. _____
47. Managers will be able to oversee more subordinates. _____
48. Some of the supervisor's responsibilities will be transferred to subordinates. _____
49. Span of control and decentralization are interrelated. _____
50. When managers are given more authority, supervisors have less work to do. _____

Diagnostic Test 2

1. We all knew Charles's speeches could be VAINGLORIOUS, but his arrogant boasting at the meeting startled even us.

   a. very glorious   c. entertaining
   b. meek   d. prideful

2. A person with top secret clearance is trusted to never DIVULGE his knowledge.

   a. hide   c. cover up
   b. give away   d. know

3. Sometimes winning an argument with one's spouse is at best a PYRRHIC VICTORY.

   a. magnificent battle   c. stunning victory
   b. crushing defeat   d. victory not worth the cost

4. Robert's wreck was the direct result of his NARCISSISM; he was watching himself in the rear-view mirror instead of watching the car in front of him.

   a. inattention   c. self-absorption
   b. stupidity   d. carelessness

5. I can eat snails in garlic sauce, but I hardly find them PALATABLE.

   a. tasty   c. indifferent
   b. displeasing   d. disgusting

6. The new employee KOWTOWED whenever the boss walked in.

   a. groveled   c. appeared indifferent
   b. spoke angrily   d. shouted

7. Joan is a FERVENT supporter of animal rights; she won't even wear leather shoes.

   a. careless   c. dedicated
   b. indifferent   d. harsh

8. The Mayor was forced to step down when his MALFEASANCE became known.

   a. wrong-doing   c. charity
   b. good-heartedness   d. humor

9. No one can watch *Old Yeller* IMPASSIVELY, it is just too heart-wrenching.

    a. sadly
    b. unemotionally
    c. quickly
    d. thoughtfully

10. There are many legends of SPECTRAL lights appearing in the windows of long-abandoned houses where violent deaths have occurred.

    a. violent
    b. ghostly
    c. unusual
    d. bright

Instructions: Write the number of the main idea sentence in the blank below each paragraph.

11. 1The only sure way to avoid "naming names" was to respond to every question by citing the Fifth Amendment to the Constitution, which protects Americans from testifying against themselves. 2When the states adopted the Fifth Amendment in 1791, they wanted to protect citizens against false confessions coerced by intimidation and torture. 3The ordeal triggered by a congressional subpoena was certainly intimidating. 4Many Americans assumed that citing the amendment was a sure sign of guilt, not a matter of principle, and talked about Fifth Amendment communists. 5"Taking the Fifth" couldn't protect jobs and reputations. (Goldfield et al., *The American Journey*)

    Main Idea _____

12. 1Criteria previously used to label a people *primitive* included the use of so-called Stone Age technology, the absence of written histories, and the failure to build "great" cities. 2Yet the accomplishments of the people of Africa strongly belie this categorization: 3Africans south of the Sahara have smelted and forged iron since at least 500 BCE, and Africans in many areas made and used high-quality steel for weapons and tools. 4Many African people have recorded their histories in Arabic since at least the tenth century. 5The first European visitors to Africa admired politically and economically sophisticated urban centers such as Benin, Luanda, and Mbanza Kongo, to name only a few. (Stokstad, *Art: A Brief History*)

    Main Idea _____

13. 1As is true for most social programs in the United States, the one providing food stamps to the needy traces its roots back to the administration of Franklin D. Roosevelt. 2In 1939, a program was implemented whereby people could purchase some food stamps and in the process, receive others free of charge. 3The former could be used for any food purchases, while the latter could be utilized only for foods that were designated as surplus commodities by the Secretary of Agriculture. 4The program, which ended in 1943, established two important precedents: 5(1) food was not free but required the recipient to pay for a portion of

its value; (2) the program benefited not only the needy recipients but the farmers who were able to dispose of surplus commodities and receive compensation. (Watson, *Promise and Performance of American Democracy*)

Main Idea _____

14. 1Anaerobic digestion of sewage sludge yields biogas, which is two-thirds methane, plus a nutrient-rich treated sludge that is a good organic fertilizer. 2Animal manure can be digested likewise. 3Where these three aspects—manure disposal, energy production, and fertilizer creation—can be combined in an efficient cycle, great economic benefit can be achieved. (Nebel & Wright, *Environmental Science*)

Main Idea _____

15. 1At the end of World War II, the major nations of the world agreed to establish fixed exchange rates. 2Under fixed exchange rates, the value of any country's currency relative to that of another country remains constant. 3Today, however, floating exchange rates are the norm, and the value of one country's currency relative to that of another varies with market conditions. 4For example, when many French citizens want to spend francs to buy U.S. dollars (or goods), the value of the dollar relative to the franc increases, or gets "stronger;" demand for the dollar is high. 5The value of the dollar thus rises with the demand for U.S. goods. 6In reality, exchange rates fluctuate by very small degrees on a daily basis. 7More significant variations usually occur over a longer time. (Ebert & Griffin, *Business Essentials*)

Main Idea _____

Instructions: Read each paragraph below, then read the three sentences underneath the paragraph. Indicate which sentence best reflects the main idea of the paragraph.

16. In contrast to the characters, the actors within this play are stiff, wooden stereotypes— obviously characters written as characters. The leading actress is full of herself and unconcerned with those around her; the leading actor is more concerned with his appearance than with his portrayal of a character; we see this when he balks at wearing a chef's hat. It is almost as if the actors have no "inner realm," whereas the characters are concerned with little else. Again this is ironic because within the realm of the play, the actors represent real people who should have more facets to their personalities. Perhaps our lack of ability to see inside the actors is one of the things that makes them seem more real.

    a. The actors in this play are very shallow, but this may add to their realism.
    b. The characters in this play have more depth than the actors.
    c. Real people should have multi-faceted personalities.

17. No work of drama is written or performed in a vacuum. Any literary work speaks to an audience, but with a play that communication is different than it is with any other form of literature. A play is not meant to be performed before a single person sitting contemplatively in a quiet room. A play may speak with a number of voices and meanings equal to the number of audience members and actors and production personnel, yet still the play is performed in a social setting, before and among a room full of people. To some extent, these people have shared an experience, have spent a moment of time together, interacting wittingly or not. This communication is reciprocal; before ever pen was set to paper, society spoke to the playwright, giving context to his life and his work.

   a. Plays are intended to be performed before a large audience.
   b. All literature is guided by social contexts and expectations.
   c. Social context is more important to a play than to any other form of literature.

18. The characters of Ibsen's *A Doll's House* begin the play by acting out what one might think of as the stereotypical nineteenth-century family scene, albeit a bit exaggerated. To the old guard among the audience, this play began in a normal, well-wrought fashion. Even to those beginning to be aware of the shifting role of women, this beginning was probably no more than a dramatized idea of the conventional ideal family.
   a. This play began in a normal, artistic fashion.
   b. At the beginning of this play, the family seemed typical for the times.
   c. The family in the first scene would soon discard convention.

19. Wemmick and his father, the "aged P," are happier than most in *Great Expectations*, but their family can hardly be called normal. Wemmick has taken the adage "a man's house is his castle" so much to heart that he has rigged a drawbridge, cannon, and other fortifications around the house. In his castle, Wemmick lives with his father, who is referred to only as the "aged Parent." Wemmick and his aged parent are proud and fond of each other and are probably the happiest family in the work.
   a. Most of the families in *Great Expectations* are unhappy.
   b. Although they are not normal, the Wemmicks are happy.
   c. Wemmick and his father live in a castle in *Great Expectations*.

20. Several of Chaucer's *Tales* exemplify the medieval attitude that life is full of pain, and even when joy is attained, it should not be expected to last. The only permanent joy is in God, and the idea of the pain of existence is apparent from the beginning of the *Tales*.
   a. Chaucer's *Tales* show his belief that life is pain.
   b. Chaucer's *Tales* demonstrate that permanent joy is only possible in the afterlife.
   c. Chaucer's *Tales* exemplify medieval attitudes about life.

Instructions: Read the passage, paying close attention to main ideas, support, and coherence. Answer the questions which follow.

1In a variant of acupuncture, a small direct electric current is run through stationary needles. 2Levitt (1981) points out that such "stimulation-produced analgesia" (SPA) has been used successfully with many pain patients suffering from cancer or nerve or brain damage. 3Activating an implanted electrode (which is an electrified "needle") for 15 to 30 minutes can provide hours of relief from pain.

1In a related method, transcutaneous electrical nerve stimulation (TENS) electrodes are attached to the skin at the site of pain. 2A mild current is passed between the electrodes across the skin. 3This method is related to SPA. 4In still another method, direct electrical stimulation is applied to the brainstem.

1Some of the effects of acupuncture, SPA, and TENS may be due to the releasing of endorphins. 2There is supportive evidence. 3The drug *naloxone* is known to block the pain-killing effects of morphine. 4The analgesic effects of SPA (Akil et al., 1976) and acupuncture are also blocked by naloxone. 5Therefore, it may well be that the analgesic effects of SPA and acupuncture can be linked to the morphine-like endorphins.

1Interestingly, the so-called placebo effect—that is, the way in which expectation of relief sometimes leads to relief from pain and other problems—has also occasionally been attributed to release of endorphins. 2In future years we may well find ways of controlling pain without drugs, acupuncture, or other external means. 3For now, there is no need to spend money on such research since we have very effective drugs. 4We may learn how to control release of our bodies' own pain-killing systems more or less directly. (Rathus, *Psychology*)

21. Which of the following sentences best states the controlling idea of this passage?_____

    a. Acupuncture is an effective way to relieve pain for hours.

    b. Despite several recent developments, the use of drugs is still the best way to reduce physical pain.

    c. The release of pain-damping endorphins can be stimulated in several ways without the use of drugs.

    d. In the future, we may be able to more readily control our own release of endorphins.

22. Which of the following sentences best states the main idea of the first paragraph?_____

    a. SPA can provide effective pain relief.

    b. Acupuncture is an effective pain reliever.

    c. Cancer patients can benefit from a form of acupuncture.

    d. SPA blocks pain by releasing endorphins.

23. What is the number of the main idea sentence of the third paragraph? _____

24. What is the number of the sentence which does not belong in the second paragraph? _____

25. What is the number of the sentence which does not belong in the fourth paragraph? _____

Instructions: Read the passage, paying close attention to main ideas, support, and coherence. Answer the questions which follow.

1Toward the end of the second year, children begin to speak in telegraphic two-word utterances. 2In the utterance "That ball," the words *is* and *a* are implied. 3There are many different types of two-word utterances, for example, agent-action ("Daddy sit"), action-object ("Hit you"), locating ("Car there"), and possessing ("Mommy cup"). 4These two-word utterances, however, do not show a grasp of syntax. 5The important thing to note is that the types of two-word utterances that tend to be used first in English also emerge first in languages as divergent as German, Russian, Luo (an African tongue), and Turkish (Slobin, 1973). 6The limited role of environmental influences can be seen as supporting the view that there is a universal, innate tendency in people to develop language according to a pre-programmed schedule. 7This view will be amplified in the section on theories of language development.

1Children's two-word utterances, while brief, nevertheless show a grasp of syntax. 2The child will say "Sit chair" to tell a parent to sit in a chair, not "Chair sit." 3(Most apes do not reliably make this distinction in ASL.) 4The child will say "My shoe," not "Shoe my," to show possession. 5"Mommy go" means Mommy is leaving, while "Go Mommy" expresses the wish for Mommy to go away. 6For this reason, "Go Mommy" is not heard frequently. 7These utterances appear to be imitative, and do not demonstrate a grasp of language. (Rathus, *Psychology*)

26. What is the number of the main idea sentence of the first paragraph? _____

27. What is the number of the main idea sentence of the second paragraph? _____

28. What is the number of the sentence which does not belong in the first paragraph? _____

29. What is the number of the sentence which does not belong in the second paragraph? _____

30. This passage supports which of the following statements?

    a. Environmental influences are the most important factors in development of language.
    b. Children go through the same stages of language development as apes.
    c. Environmental influences play only a limited role in language development.
    d. Apes cannot be taught language.

Tone and Bias

Instructions: Read the following paragraphs. Answer the questions following each one.
Fencing was an immediate problem, for crops needed to be shielded from livestock. But without timber, farmers could not build wooden fences. Barbed wire, developed in the mid-1870s, solved the problem. By 1900, farmers were importing nearly 300 million pounds of barbed wire each year from eastern and midwestern factories. (Goldfield, et. al., *The American Journey*)

31. The author's tone is _____.

    a. persuasive   c. neutral
    b. defensive   d. negative

32.   The author is strongly biased in favor of _____.
    a. wooden fences c. barbed wire
    b. not apparent   d. ranchers

Critics have charged that the mantle of human rights cloaks the pursuit of less noble U.S. interests in other nations. Whether or not this critique is valid, it is clear that as the twenty-first century dawns, any interventionist foreign policy must present itself in the idealistic terms of a special American mission if it is to have public support. (Goldfield, et. al., *The American Journey*)

33. The author's tone is _____.

    a. persuasive   c. neutral
    b. defensive   d. negative

34. The author is strongly biased in favor of _____.

    a. interventionism   c. human rights
    b. not apparent   d. American missions

For the temperance crusade to succeed, old forms of cultural and social behavior had to be abandoned and new ones learned. The reformers had to demonize alcohol and then banish it from the household and workplace. They had to finance a massive propaganda campaign and link it to an organization that could mobilize and energize thousands of people. They built such a mass movement by merging temperance into the network of churches and lay volunteers that the benevolent empire (The United States) had developed and by adopting the techniques of revivals to win new converts. (Goldfield, et. al., *The American Journey*)

35. The author's tone is _____.

    a. persuasive   c. neutral
    b. not apparent d. somewhat critical

36. The author is biased against _____.

    a. the temperance crusade   c. alcohol
    b. not apparent   d. churches

Smoking has not been proven harmful, and smokers should not be segregated in restaurants and public buildings. I have never seen smoking hurt anyone. My father smoked until he was 71, and he was never sick a day in his life.

37. The author's tone is _____.

    a. persuasive   c. neutral
    b. defensive   d. critical

38. The author is biased against _____.

    a. smoking   c. smoke-free businesses
    b. not apparent d. nonsmokers

Values-based stewardship is a call to life-changing stewardship put within the value system of a community. In this case, putting the call within the context of the faith of the watermen resulted in the establishment of structures within the community that show great promise in helping to bring the entire island community toward a sustainable future. (Nebel & Wright, *Environmental Science*)

39. The author's tone is _____.

    a. admiring   c. neutral
    b. cautionary   d. negative

40. The author is strongly biased in favor of _____.

    a. watermen   c. value systems
    b. not apparent d. stewardship

Reading Rate

Instructions: Read the passage; the computer will time you as you read. When you are finished, press "enter" and answer the questions.

The Myth of Objective Science (Nebel & Wright, *Environmental Science*)

The image of the white-coated scientist is a familiar and reassuring one. Scientific evidence now provides the foundation for many important public debates, including those in environmental management. But how accurate is the image of the scientist as an objective seeker of truth?

Scientific analysis is not just a straightforward process of observation and reporting but, rather, a complex series of personal decisions, value judgments, and guesses, influenced by the scientist's unique combination of personal experiences, fears, hopes, desires, and values. Like the rest of us, scientists worry about their careers, their families, and their finances. Ultimately, these human qualities influence the ways that individuals see and interpret scientific information. For this reason, it is not uncommon for two scientists to examine the same data set but reach very different conclusions.

Beth Savan, in her book *Science Under Siege*, cites the example of Stephen Jay Gould, a professor of geology at Harvard University. Gould reanalyzed data compiled by Samuel Morton, a nineteenth-century physician, on the physical and intellectual differences among human races. Gould's analysis showed that Morton had consciously or unconsciously manipulated his data to arrive at the conclusion—widely held when Morton was alive—that white people are a superior race. Yet in his own analysis, Gould misread one of Morton's figures, leading him to underestimate racial differences in the data and thus to arrive at a conclusion more in keeping with his own preconceptions—that the differences among races are small.

This example demonstrates another feature of scientific analysis—that we tend to favor familiar, widely accepted views, while demanding a higher standard of proof for new ideas. Sometimes these biases can create obstacles to sound decision making. For example, a group of Western scientists planned to conserve Peary caribou in the High Arctic by protecting females and juveniles but allowing some hunting of adult males. Inuit hunters, knowledgeable about the social structure of caribou herds, warned that this practice would instead speed the decline of the population. Subsequent monitoring has confirmed the validity of their position.

Human emotions and values underlie most of the environmental disputes of this century. Divergent scientific analyses are often seen in the development of environmental standards. Environmental managers can reveal these subjective influences and make them explicit in decision making by including a wide range of viewpoints in their analysis and by recognizing and, where possible, compensating for their own unique values and biases.

Word Count: 413   Minutes: _____   Rate: _____

41. T or F Scientists are objective seekers of truth.
42. T or F It is common for two scientists to examine the same evidence and reach different conclusions.

43. Science is _____.

   a. influenced by personal decisions and guesses
   b. worried about careers, families, and finances
   c. a complex series of decisions, judgments, and guesses

44. Two examples of scientists who misinterpreted data are _____.

   a. Savan and Gould
   b. Morton and Gould
   c. Morton and Savan

45. T or F Beth Savan, in her book *Science Under Siege,* demonstrates that the differences among races are small.

Instructions: After reading the paragraph below, label the following details as Main Idea (MI), Major Detail (MJ), or Minor Detail (MN).

In addition to easing the way into new markets, alliances give firms greater control over their foreign activities than independent agents and licensing arrangements. (At the same time, of course, all partners in an alliance retain some say in its decisions.) Perhaps most important, alliances allow firms to benefit from the knowledge and expertise of their foreign partners. The importance of such knowledge in Japan, for instance, has prompted all but a handful of U.S. companies to do business there through alliances. For example, Petrofsky's International, a St. Louis maker of frozen bagel dough, encountered trouble with health officials when it first tried to market its product in Japan. Food inspectors objected to the fact that yeast—an essential ingredient—was an "active bacteria." Petrofsky entered an alliance with Itochu, a giant Japanese importer, who managed to get the product certified. (Ebert & Griffin, *Business Essentials*)

46. Petrofsky's entered an alliance with Itochu. _____
47. Alliances allow firms to benefit from the knowledge of their partners. _____
48. Petrofsky's encountered trouble when it tried to market its product in Japan. _____
49. Most U.S. companies doing business in Japan use alliances. _____
50. Alliances are beneficial in many ways to participant firms. _____

Diagnostic Test 3

1. My math teachers spent many hours trying to KINDLE in me an interest in algebra.

   a. interest   c. eliminate
   b. create   d. multiply

2. Miss Brown's manner toward students lives up to her reputation; one does not want to make a mistake that could lead to being on the receiving end of her CHASTISEMENT.

   a. kindness   c. punishment
   b. hatred   d. rudeness

3. My two-year-old son Carlos says whatever comes into his mind, but his twin brother Jamie only PARROTS whatever I say.

   a. repeats   c. chirps
   b. invents   d. laughs at

4. He traveled across the PAMPAS for five years. The level grassy plains often provided a breathtaking view.

   a. road   c. cities
   b. flat lands   d. mountains

5. His article on orchids is DEFINITIVE - it has everything you might want to know about these flowers.

   a. comprehensive c. final
   b. long   d. ordinary

6. My argument is based on very reliable PREMISES.

   a. land   c. suppositions
   b. property   d. falsehoods

7. The thought of taking the higher paying job was a TANTALIZING thought to Mary; however, she chose to continue her education.

   a. tempting   c. final
   b. valuable   d. stimulating

8. It took many months to rid ourselves of the DETRITUS left after the tornado had swept through the center of town.

   a. trash
   b. fuel
   c. storm shelters
   d. valuable items

9. John's STENTORIAN bellow when he discovered the snake in his sleeping bag woke the whole camp.

   a. muffled
   b. hesitant
   c. loud
   d. operatic

10. They were RELUCTANT to enter the abandoned building after dark.

    a. happy
    b. hesitant
    c. cheerful
    d. sad

Instructions: Write the number of the main idea sentence in the blank below each paragraph.

11. 1Eventually the Supreme Court ruled in *Commonwealth v. Hunt* (1842) that union activities were not illegal per se, but depended on the *objectives* of the unions and the *means* used to accomplish those objectives. 2However, this decision did not usher in a new era of prolabor policy. 3Employers were free to use the tactics described above (yellow-dog contracts, discharges, blacklists, lockouts) to combat unions and to engage labor spies and strikebreakers. 4Police were often used to prevent unions from meeting and to help drive union organizers out of town. 5On some occasions federal troops intervened in labor disputes, usually on the grounds that violence was threatened; 6such intervention typically resulted in the suppression of a strike and victory for the employers. (Watson, *Promise and Performance of American Democracy*)

    Main Idea _____

12. 1Throughout much of history, wind power—in addition to propelling sailing ships—was widely used for grinding grain, hence the term windmill. 2Then, wind-driven propellers went on to perform other tasks. 3Until the 1940s, most farms in the United States used windmills for pumping water and generating small amounts of electricity. 4In the '30s and '40s, windmills fell into disuse, however, as transmission lines brought abundant lower-cost power from central generating plants. 5Not until the energy crisis and rising energy costs of the '70s did wind begin to be seriously considered again as a potential source of sustainable energy. (Nebel & Wright, *Environmental Science*)

    Main Idea _____

13. 1A few years ago, Hyatt Hotels checked 379 employees into the chain's 98 hotels. 2They were not, however, treated as guests. 3Rather, they were asked to make beds, carry luggage, and perform the other tasks necessary to make a big hotel function. 4Top management at Hyatt believes that learning more about the work of lower-level employees will allow executives to understand them better as human beings (and coworkers). (Ebert & Griffin, *Business Essentials*)

Main Idea _____

14. 1Functional analysis serves a number of purposes. 2It makes you more aware of the environmental context of your behavior. 3It can increase your motivation to change, and it can lead to significant behavioral change. 4In studies with highly motivated people, functional analysis alone has been found to increase the amount of time spent studying (Johnson & White, 1971) or talking in a therapy group (Komaki & Dore-Boyce, 1978), and to decrease the number of cigarettes smoked (Lipinski et al., 1975). (Rathus, *Psychology*)

Main Idea _____

15. 1What can you learn from studying fossils selected from ten million generations of horses? 2First, you can see that horses gradually changed over a long period of time. 3Second, these changes were orderly and resulted in variations that seem to have enabled the horse to adapt to new environments. 4Here once more is evidence to support Darwin's theory of natural selection. 5The evolutionary sequence of the horse is not unique in geologic history. 6Similar lines have been established for elephants, camels, and many invertebrate animals. (Bisque & Heller, *Investigating the Earth*)

Main Idea _____

Instructions: Read each paragraph below, then read the three sentences underneath the paragraph. Indicate which sentence best reflects the main idea of the paragraph.

16. In the 1700s, the emphasis in literature was still strongly Neo-classical and concerned with man and his artifacts ruling over and imposing order on the world. With the emergence of the Romantics a new appreciation of untouched natural beauty arose. This new paradigm influenced the subsequent realistic writers of the early twentieth century. One other influential aspect of this span of British history and literature was the Industrial Revolution. The emergence of multitudes of manufactories and sweatshops, and of industries that supported these businesses with raw materials, enhanced the sensitivity of writers to their relatively untouched natural surroundings.

    a. Writers shifted emphasis from manmade artifacts to natural beauty between the eighteenth and twentieth centuries.
    b. Literature in the 1700s was man-centered and showed little concern for nature.
    c. The Industrial Revolution strongly influenced British literature.

17. One of the features of the *Oxford English Dictionary* is the etymology information. This extra information makes the dictionary quite large and undoubtedly adds to its intimidating appearance. You will find, however, that if you will spend some time perusing the thing, you will not have wasted your time. The *OED*'s features make common words more interesting. They also make it easier to remember the new words and add them to your vocabulary.

    a. The *OED* is quite intimidating and very large.
    b. The *OED* is worth perusing for several reasons.
    c. Reading the *OED* will improve your vocabulary.

18. Where the realists were trying to capture the external world, the surrealists were trying to capture the world inside. Where the realists tried to convey passion and meaning through choice of subject matter and placement of objects on the canvas, the surrealists distorted the objects themselves to reflect the message of the painting. The realists tried to copy objects in nature. Surrealists tried to make objects in nature copy them.

    a. Surrealist paintings are deliberately distorted to reflect internal forces.
    b. Realist artists tried to paint objects as they appeared.
    c. The surrealists rejected realism in several ways.

19. Greek columns may be seen on many modern courthouses across the nation. Classical arches formed of concrete decorate many new church buildings. Even gargoyles can be seen squatting on several modern buildings in New York.

    a. Many classical architectural adornments are still popular today.
    b. Government buildings often reflect classical elements of architecture.
    c. Many classical elements of architecture serve to strengthen modern buildings.

20. Mayan civilization was in decline by the time of the Spanish Conquest. By the end of the fifteenth century, a people known as the Aztecs were rulers of much of Mexico. Their rise to power had been recent and swift. Only 400 years earlier, according to their own legends, they had been a nomadic people living on the shores of the mythological island called Aztlan somewhere to the northwest of the Valley of Mexico, where present-day Mexico City is located. They called themselves the Mexica, hence the name Mexico. The term Aztec derives from the word Aztlan. (Stokstad, *Art: A Brief History*)

    a. The Aztecs ruled much of Mexico after the Mayan influence declined.
    b. Mayan civilization was destroyed by the Spanish Conquest.
    c. The Aztecs began as a nomadic people on the shores of Aztlan.

Instructions: Read the passage, paying close attention to main ideas, support, and coherence. Answer the questions which follow.

1What factors contribute to creativity? 2Guilford (1959) has noted that creative people show flexibility, fluency (in generating words and ideas), and originality. 3Getzels and Jackson (1962) found that creative schoolchildren tend to express rather than inhibit their feelings, and to be playful and independent. 4Conger and Petersen (1984) concur that creative people tend to be independent and nonconformist. 5Teachers, however, do not encourage independence. 6But independence and nonconformity do not necessarily make a person creative. 7Stereotypes of the creative personality have led to individual exaggerations of nonconformity.

1Nevertheless, creative children are often at odds with their teachers because of their independence. 2Faced with the chore of managing upwards of 30 pupils, teachers too often label quiet and submissive children as "good" children. 3These studies of creativity may also explain in part why there have been many more male than female artists throughout history, even though Maccoby and Jacklin (1974) found no sex differences in creativity. 4Female artists are not generally as creative as their male counterparts. 5As Conger and Petersen (1984) point out, traits like independence and nonconformity are more likely to be discouraged in females than in males, because such traits are inconsistent with the passive and compliant social roles traditionally ascribed to females. 6Because of the women's movement, the numbers of women in the creative arts and sciences are growing rapidly today. 7In the past the creativity of many girls may have been nipped in the bud. (Rathus, *Psychology*)

21. Which of the following sentences best states the controlling idea of this passage?

    a. Males tend to be more creative than females because of greater independence.
    b. Creative people, male and female, tend to be independent and nonconformist.
    c. There are no inherent sex differences in creativity.
    d. The numbers of creative women are growing rapidly.

22. Which of the following statements best reflects the main idea of the first paragraph?
    a. Creative people often seem odd.
    b. Much research has been done to determine what leads to creativity.
    c. Creative people often suffer from being stereotyped.
    d. There are many traits which seem characteristic of creative people.

23. What is the number of the main idea sentence of the second paragraph? _____

24. What is the number of the sentence which does not belong in the first paragraph? _____

25. What is the number of the sentence which does not belong in the second paragraph? _____

1Another social motive is the need for power (*n* Power)—the need to control organizations and other people. 2Low-*n*-Power college students are less likely to be noticed by administrators. 3High-*n*-Power college students are more likely than others to be members of important committees and to hold prominent offices in student organizations (Beck, 1978).

4They are more likely than low-*n*-Power individuals to participate in aggressive contact sports and to seek out competitive careers, as in business and—interestingly—psychology.

1 Group leaders are high-*n*-Power individuals. 2The need for power has both its positive and negative features, since power can be used either for good or bad purposes. 3In one recent study it was found that group leaders with a high need for power may impede group decision making by failing to promote full discussion of all the facts concerning a business situation and by not encouraging full consideration of members' proposals (Fodor & Smith, 1982).

1McClelland and Pilon (1983) found that high-*n*-Power adults were more likely than low-*n*-Power adults to have had parents who were permissive toward their children's sexual and aggressive behavior. 2That is, they were more likely to permit their children to masturbate, to engage in sex play, and to show aggression to their siblings and their parents. 3These people let their kids get away with practically anything. 4Perhaps allowing children to exercise power (to control themselves and others) at an early age encourages them to continue to exercise power as they develop. (Rathus, *Psychology*)

26. What is the number of the main idea sentence of the second paragraph? _____

27. What is the number of the main idea sentence of the third paragraph? _____

28. What is the number of the sentence which does not belong in the first paragraph? _____

29. What is the number of the sentence which does not belong in the second paragraph? _____

30. What is the number of the sentence which does not belong in the third paragraph? _____

Instructions: Read the following paragraphs. Answer the questions following each one.

1Now that we have a Republican leader again, the U.S. can look forward to broad, positive changes in its situation. Businesses will gain the tax incentives they need to develop new products and employ more people. Law abiding citizens will be protected and criminals punished as they should be. Our troops can finally be pulled out of countries where they have no business in the first place

31. The author's tone is _____.

    a. critical   c. neutral
    b. cautionary   d. upbeat

32. The author is strongly biased against _____.

    a. Democrats   c. Republicans
    b. not apparent   d. politicians

Students in mathematics need a great deal of practice in order to understand the concepts being taught. That is why they must be given large amounts of homework every night. There is no other way to develop the appropriate skills.

33. The author's tone is _____.

    a. persuasive   c. neutral
    b. cautionary   d. negative

34. The author is strongly biased in favor of _____.

    a. students   c. homework
    b. not apparent   d. mathematics

Research has shown that copious homework is an effective way for students to develop math skills. There may be other methods that work, but homework is a familiar, time-tested way to help students grasp new math concepts. Therefore, before I switch to a new method, I want to see evidence of its effectiveness

35. The author's tone is _____.

    a. persuasive   c. neutral
    b. reasonable   d. negative

36.The author is strongly biased in favor of _____.

    a. students   c. homework
    b. not apparent   d. mathematics

Arnold Schwarzenegger is truly one of the greatest figures in Hollywood today. He is great not so much for his questionable acting ability, but for the breadth and scope of his achievements. He was Mr. Olympia seven times; he is one of the highest paid actors in Hollywood; he headed the President's Council on Physical Fitness for several years; and he has co-authored a number of successful books. When he came to this country, he couldn't even speak English. His drive and determination are remarkable.

37.The author's tone is _____.

    a. persuasive   c. neutral
    b. defensive   d. admiring

38.The author is strongly biased in favor of _____.

    a. actors   c. Hollywood
    b. not apparent   d. Arnold

The desire of the new immigrants to retain their cultural traditions led contemporary observers to doubt their ability to assimilate into American society. Even sympathetic observers, such as social workers, marveled at the utterly foreign character of immigrant districts. (Goldfield, et. al., *The American Journey*)

39. The author's tone is _____.

   a. persuasive   c. neutral
   b. defensive   d. negative

40. The author is strongly biased against _____.

   a. assimilation   c. immigrants
   b. not apparent   d. social workers

Reading Rate

Instructions: Read the passage; the computer will time you as you read. When you are finished, press "enter" and answer the questions.

Genetic Diversity and Measuring Species Change (Nebel & Wright, *Environmental Science*)

Genetic diversity within a species has been compared to a baseball team. If you only have a catcher and some outfielders, you do not have enough diversity to make a viable team. And if your "pool" of players doesn't contain the necessary components—for instance, good pitchers— it is impossible to create a winning team. Similarly, gene pools must be diverse enough to support a self-sustaining population. If diversity is low, the population of a species runs the risk of declining rapidly or becoming extinct. For this reason, environmental managers now track genetic diversity carefully in managed populations and constantly evaluate the significance of change for the viability of the species overall. One way that environmental managers track genetic diversity is through population genetics. Population genetics is a powerful tool currently used to define a species and its characteristics. Using "marker" genes, geneticists can quickly identify specific DNA sequences that are unique to a particular population. In this way, scientists can track the genetic origins of a given population—and determine when significant change has occurred locally and in the species overall.

This technique has been especially important in aquaculture, where genetically engineered populations of native species such as salmon or carp may be "farmed" in large tanks or in ocean enclosures. Occasionally, farmed fish escape and interbreed with native populations, producing offspring with genetics that reflect both parent populations. Although native and farmed individuals may appear identical, they may differ in their growth potential and other important characteristics, such as resistance to disease. Because wild populations provide a valuable reservoir of genetic diversity, it is important that they be conserved, both for their inherent value and as a rich gene pool that can be used to augment farmed populations.

Genetic analysis is also helpful in determining the potential for extinction of a population or species. For instance, anecdotal evidence from Acadia National Park, Maine, suggested that the native beaver population was eradicated a hundred years ago. Beavers are still observed in the park, although recent studies reveal a dramatic decline in numbers—perhaps as much as 60 percent in the last 15 years. Genetic analysis has demonstrated that the beavers now living in the park are descended from two or three pairs introduced from the Mid-Atlantic states. The low genetic diversity in this population—a result of the small gene pool of ancestors—may be a factor in the current population decline, as well as an indication of the beaver's increased potential for extinction.

Word Count: 425   Minutes: _____   Rate: _____

41. This passage compares genetic diversity to a _____.

    a. football team
    b. soccer team
    c. baseball team

42. T or F   According to the passage, if a species' gene pool is not as diverse as a sports team, the species will die out.

43. Environmental managers track genetic diversity through _____.

    a. population genetics
    b. genetic diversity
    c. genetic origins

44. Tracking genetic diversity is particularly important in _____.
    a. agriculture
    b. bioculture
    c. aquaculture

45. Native and farmed individuals may differ in _____.

    a. growth potential
    b. resistance to disease
    c. a and b

Instructions: After reading the paragraph below, label the following details as Main Idea (MI), Major Detail (MJ), or Minor Detail (MN).

    An **independent agent** is a foreign individual or organization that agrees to represent an exporter's interests in foreign markets. Independent agents often act as sales representatives: they sell the exporter's products, collect payment, and make sure that customers are satisfied. Independent agents often represent several firms at once and usually do not specialize in a particular product or market. Levi-Strauss uses agents to market clothing products in many small countries in Africa, Asia, and South America. (Ebert & Griffin, *Business Essentials*)

46. Independent agents represent several firms at once. _____

47. An Independent agent represents an exporter's interests in foreign markets. _____

48. Levi-Strauss uses agents to market clothing products in many small countries. _____

49. Independent agents sell exporter's products, collect payment, and ensure customer satisfaction. _____

50. Independent agents act as sales representatives. _____

Answer Key

Diagnostic Test 1

1. c
2. a
3. a
4. a
5. b
6. b
7. c
8. a
9. c
10. b
11. 4
12. 4
13. 5
14. 3
15. 1
16. b
17. c
18. c
19. b
20. b
21. a
22. 3
23. 4
24. 4
25. 3
26. 1
27. 4
28. 6
29. 2
30. c
31. d
32. c
33. b
34. a
35. a
36. b
37. b
38. a
39. d
40. a
41. b
42. c

43. t
44. F
45. a
46. mn
47. mj
48. mj
49. mi
50. mj

Diagnostic Test 2

1. d
2. b
3. d
4. c
5. a
6. a
7. c
8. a
9. b
10. b
11. 1
12. 2
13. 4
14. 3
15. 3
16. a
17. a
18. b
19. b
20. c
21. b
22. a
23. 5
24. 2
25. 3
26. 3
27. 1
28. 6
29. 6
30. a
31. a
32. c
33. a
34. b

35. b
36. a
37. b
38. c
39. a
40. a
41. f
42. t
43. a
44. b
45. f
46. mn
47. mj
48. mn
49. mn
50. mi

Diagnostic Test 3

1. b
2. c
3. a
4. b
5. a
6. c
7. a
8. a
9. c
10. c
11. 3
12. 2
13. 4
14. 1
15. 4
16. a
17. b
18. c
19. a
20. c
21. b
22. d
23. 3
24. 5
25. 2
26. 2
27. 1

28. 2
29. 1
30. 3
31. d
32. a
33. b
34. d
35. a
36. c
37. d
38. d
39. a
40. b
41. c
42. t
43. a
44. c
45. c
46. mj
47. mi
48. mn
49. mj
50. mj

The following tests were taken from

Hughes, Suzanne E. and Levine-Brown, Patti. *The Prentice Hall Exit Test Study Guide for Reading*. Upper Saddle River, N.J. 2005.1-9,117-126.

Pretest

Read each passage and answer the questions.

Passage 1

1   One of the most famous of the cromlechs, a monumental stone structure made of huge blocks of boulders used singly or in groups, that was used for religious rites is Stonehenge in Southern England. What we see today is the result of several distinct building campaigns, beginning in the New Stone Age and continuing into the early Bronze Age.

5   During the first phase, from roughly 3500 to 2900 B.C., a nearly continuous circle was dug into the chalk ground. A silted ditch was added about 3300-2140 B.C. and then the avenue down to the Avon River sometime from 2580 to 1890 B.C. The sandstone circle of evenly spaced trilithons, each consisting of two upright posts and a horizontal slab, was erected during the early Bronze Age Wessex culture between 2850 and 2200 B.C. These immense

10   stones were evidently dragged from Marlborough Downs, some twenty miles away—a feat as awesome as raising them, but it is a far from clear whether the inner bluestone circle and horseshoe, which date from several hundred years later (2480-1940 B.C.), were deposited by glaciers or carried by carts and rafts from the Preseli Mountains in Wales some two hundred miles to the west. During the final phase, from 2030 to 1520 B.C., this

15   arrangement was echoed in two similarly marked circles and a smaller horseshoe that enclose an altar like stone at the center.

    Why was Stonehenge built in the first place? The widely held belief that the so-called Heel Stone was positioned so that the sun would rise directly above it on the day of the summer solstice, when the sun is farthest from the equator, has long been shown to be

20   incorrect. It appears that Stonehenge was originally aligned with the major and minor moonrises. Only later, did the structure become oriented toward the sun; the Heel Stone and fallen "Slaughter Stone", along with other stones and the alignment of the causeway were rearranged in the direction of the summer sunrise.

    Each of Stonehenge's building phases was linked to broader changes during the

25   Neolithic and Bronze Ages. Burial mounds and prehistoric monuments made of circles of massive stones from as early as 3500 B.C. that have been found in Scandinavia and northern Britain reflect the changeover to a settled, agrarian way of life. However, the people who created the Wessex culture probably crossed the English Channel from Brittany in northwestern France, where massive horseshoes made of enormous stones

30   constructed with astronomical arrangements are far more common than in England. They brought with them Bronze Age technologies and ideas that must have seemed revolutionary to the local population, who initially put up a stiff resistance. In Stonehenge and elsewhere in southern England, these newcomers imposed their own traditions on established practices. In addition to erecting even large circles of mammoth stones, they buried their

35   leaders in burial mounds lined with boulders and used a rudimentary form of a burial chamber in the tombs. Stonehenge was eventually abandoned about 1000 B.C., as part of another change that occurred during the last Bronze Age; the preference for cremation over

burials for the dead became popular at that time.

(Adapted from Janson, H. W. and Anthony F. *A Basic History of Art, 6th ed.* Upper Saddle River, N.J: Prentice Hall. 2003. 44–45)

1. The implied main idea of the second paragraph is that

   A. Stonehenge was built to align specific stones with the position of the sun at the summer solstice, the time when the sun is farthest from the earth.
   B. Stonehenge is thought to have originally been positioned to align with the moonrises and the sun's positions throughout the year.
   C. Stonehenge appears to have been built to align with the major and minor moonrises and did not align with the solstice sun until later in time.
   D. The Heel Stone was positioned so that the sun would rise directly above it on the day of the summer solstice (when the sun is farthest from the equator).

2. According to the passage, the silted ditch was added before

   A. the original sandstone circle of evenly spaced trilithons.
   B. the nearly continuous circle in the chalk ground in Southern England was dug.
   C. the blue sandstone stones were dragged from Marlborough Downs.
   D. two marked circles and a small horseshoe near the altar like stone were built.

3. For this passage, the author uses an overall organizational pattern of

   A. simple listing.
   B. time order.
   C. cause effect.
   D. spatial order.

4. The author's primary purpose in the passage is to

   A. praise Stonehenge for its uniqueness.
   B. argue that Stonehenge is not that important because there are many similar structures.
   C. explain the phases Stonehenge went through before it was abandoned.
   D. describe the cromlech Stonehenge's appearance.

5. The implied relationship between the sentences of paragraph 3 (lines 32–35) is

   "In Stonehenge and elsewhere in southern England, these newcomers imposed their own traditions on established practices. In addition to erecting even larger circles of mammoth stones, they buried their leaders in burial mounds lined with boulders and used a rudimentary form of a burial chamber in the tombs."

   A. simple listing.
   B. spatial order.
   C. example.

D. contrast.

6. The relationship between the sentences of paragraph 3 (lines 25–30) is

    A. comparison.
    B. contrast.
    C. spatial order.
    D. order of importance.

7. "These immense stones were evidently dragged from Marlborough Downs, some twenty miles away—a feat as awesome as raising them, but it is a far from clear whether the inner bluestone circle and horseshoe, which date from several hundred years later (2480-1940 B.C.), were deposited by glaciers or carried by carts and rafts from the Preseli mountains in Wales some 200 miles to the west." (lines 9–14)

    The above sentence is a statement of

    A. fact.
    B. opinion.

8. As used in line 31, the word "technologies" means

    A. electrical machines.
    B. skills and tools.
    C. gas powered tools.
    D. traditions.

9. A conclusion that can be drawn from this passage is that

    A. the modifications in Stonehenge reflect the changes in the culture of the time.
    B. until recently it was widely believed that Stonehenge was originally built to be lined up with the moonrises.
    C. the desire for burials led to the desertion of Stonehenge.
    D. people must have figured out a way to transport the stones from the inner bluestone circle and horseshoe.

Passage 2

1   The average student spends a lot of time thinking about his or her body and ways to make it more attractive. While most people realize that there are a wide range of body types and sizes, attractiveness tends to be more narrowly defined by the images of men and women we see in the popular media; and nearly all media images equate attractiveness and
5   desirability with a limited range of body types.
     For men, the image of a tall, broad-shouldered, muscular man with so little body fat that every muscle is visible is portrayed as most desirable.
     The standards for female beauty are unforgiving also. Images of female beauty are almost exclusively women with small hips; long, thin limbs; large breasts; and no body fat.
10   This is virtually the only image of female beauty seen in fashion magazines, on billboards, on television, and in the movies.

Into this milieu steps the average college students—worried about appearance, trying to find time to study, exercise, and socialize and now making all his or her own decisions about food, often on a limited budget.

15 Making choices that are good for long-term health is not easy. The typical dining-center meal-plan choices, often greasy and fat-laden, are available in unlimited portions. The difficulty of making healthful choices is compounded by the presence of campus snack shops, vending machines, and conveniently located fast-food restaurants that offer time-pressed students easily accessible, inexpensive foods containing little nutrition. Coupling

20 tremendous pressure to be thin with a glut of readily available unhealthful foods can lead to the establishment of unhealthful eating habits that persist far beyond college life. In many cases, these conflicting pressures can lead students to develop eating habits that result in a lifelong battle with obesity or starvation, along with their associated health risks.

(Material in this passage was adapted from Belk, Colleen and Virginia Borden. *Biology Science for Life. 1st ed.* Upper Saddle River, NJ: Prentice Hall, 2004. 23)

10. The implied main idea for paragraph one is that

A. the media's idea of beauty and allure encompasses few body types and few different viewpoints.
B. the media equates attractiveness and desirability with being a beautiful college student.
C. college students spend a lot of time thinking about making their bodies look attractive as it is portrayed in the media.
D. many people realize that beauty can encompass a wide variety of body shapes and types, which is unlike the media viewpoints of beauty.

11. The author's primary purpose in the passage is to

A. entertain the reader with some facts about college students and their beliefs about their bodies.
B. persuade you about the effect of the media's images of beauty on college students.
C. narrate a story about college students' ideas of beauty.
D. praise the effects of the media's idea of beauty on the college students.

12. According to the passage, the media's versions of the ideal attractive woman and man

A. have visible muscles.
B. are possible for most people to achieve.
C. are considered beautiful by all people.
D. have little or no body fat.

13. "Coupling tremendous pressure to be thin with a glut of readily available unhealthful foods can lead to the establishment of unhealthful eating habits that persist far beyond college life." (lines 19–21)

The relationship of the parts within the sentence above is

   A. cause effect.
   B. spatial order.
   C. time order.
   D. illustration and example.

14. In this passage, the author expresses a biased attitude against

   A. unattractive people.
   B. media images of beauty.
   C. college students.
   D. healthy food.

15. The tone of this passage can best be described as

   A. impartial.
   B. sensationalistic.
   C. ambivalent.
   D. aggrieved.

16. A conclusion that can be drawn from this passage is

   A. the media's presentation of attractiveness can influence college students far into their future.
   B. college students pay little attention to the media's presentation of attractiveness because they have little time to view the media.
   C. all college students' eating problems relate to trying to lose weight because they wish to look like the media's image of beauty.
   D. broad-shouldered, muscular men that are average height are not desirable or attractive to college students.

17. "The typical dining-center meal-plan choices, often greasy and fat-laden, are available in unlimited portions." (lines 15–16)

The above sentence is a statement of
   A. fact.
   B. opinion.

18. The author's claim that "making choices that are good for long-term health is not easy" (line 15) is

   A. adequately supported by examples.
   B. inadequately supported because of lack of evidence.

Passage 3

1   On rainy days at certain times of the year, an unusual sight can be seen in southern
Florida. Schools of grayish fish with long, firm barbels known as "walking catfish" migrate
across highways when the food supply in their habitat is exhausted; occasionally many of
them are run over and the road becomes slick with the fish guts. These atypical fish have
5   structures called arborescent organs, which allow them to utilize oxygen from the air, unlike
fish whose lung like structures would collapse in the absence of water's buoyancy.
     The introduction of "walking catfish" to the United States took place in the middle to the
twentieth century when fish being transported to aquacultural farms in South Florida
somehow escaped and entered the local waterways. They propagated rapidly and spread
10   through the area where they drastically affected the environments in which they lived.
Walking catfish, Clarias batrachus, are voracious eaters who will eat fish eggs, larvae,
insects, crustaceans, and even debris found in the silt at the bottom of the water. Some of
the fish migrated to aquaculture farms where they devoured the populations of fish, which
created financial problems for the owner and a shortfall for the farmer's restaurants and food
15   preparation customers. When they consumed the food in one body of water, they moved to
a new pond or lake and consumed all the native fish and food in the environment. The fish
then moved to another body of water by wiggling themselves along the ground with the aid
of their pectoral spines and by breathing through their unusual lung like structures. They
decimated local fish populations in the Intercoastal Waterway and in many Florida lakes,
20   ponds, streams, and canals and created tribulations for commercial fishermen.
     Luckily, the Clarias batrachus does not survive in cold water, so environmentalists hope
the spread of these detrimental catfish will slow as the fish reach waterways with colder
water. There is some concern that the fish will survive short cold spells by burrowing in the
mud, by finding warm springs, or by mutating to a form that can endure the cold. Only time
25   will tell what will happen to these strange and unusual fish.

19. The implied main idea for this passage is

   A. the "walking catfish" can move across land when it needs to find a new home because it
      has arborescent organs which allow it to obtain oxygen from the air, unlike most other
      fish.
   B. because the "walking catfish" can move across land, it is decimating fish populations and
      causing problems for many people as it spreads across Florida.
   C. people who own fish farms are experiencing financial difficulties when the "walking
      catfish" eats their product.
   D. the "walking catfish" bodies can be a traffic hazard on some of the Floridian highways
      during certain times of year.

20. According to the passage, at the present time, the "walking catfish"

   A. need warm water to survive.
   B. find warm mud to hide in.
   C. live only in warm springs.
   D. are finicky eaters.

21. The author's primary purpose in the passage is to

   A. inform people about the "walking catfish."
   B. entertain the reader with a story about an unusual fish.
   C. criticize the manner in which the "walking catfish" has been treated.
   D. evaluate the financial difficulties caused by the "walking catfish."

22. The second paragraph is organized by

   A. listing the "walking catfish's" characteristics and eating habits.
   B. listing the events that took place after the "walking catfish" was introduced to Florida.
   C. providing reasons for the financial problems the 'walking catfish" creates.
   D. summarizing the life cycle of the 'walking catfish."

23. "These atypical fish have structures called arborescent organs, which allow them to utilize oxygen from the air, unlike fish whose lung like structures would collapse in the absence of water's buoyancy." (lines 4–6)

   The relationship of parts within the sentences of above is

   A. cause effect.
   B. comparison.
   C. contrast.
   D. illustration and example.

24. As used in line 9, the word "propagated" means

   A. broadcast.
   B. bred.
   C. moved.
   D. walked.

25. The tone of this passage can best be described as

   A. impartial.
   B. playful.
   C. instructive.
   D. encouraging.

26. An inference that can be drawn from this passage is

   A. if the "walking catfish" continues to spread, there will be no fish left.
   B. if the "walking catfish" can burrow in the mud to keep warm, they may continue to spread into different areas.
   C. if the "walking catfish" mutates, they will definitely be able to live outside the water for longer periods.
   D. because the "walking catfish" can breathe outside of the water, it does not need water to breed.

27. In this passage, the author expresses a biased attitude against

   A. fish.
   B. commercial fishermen.
   C. aquaculture farm owners.
   D. the "walking catfish."

Passage 4

1   The stomach secretes hydrochloric acid to aid in the digestion of food. Sometimes overindulgence or emotional stress leads to a condition of hyperacidity (too much acid). Hundreds of brands of antacids are sold in the United States to treat this condition. Despite the many brand names, there are only a few different antacid ingredients, all of which are

5   bases. Common ingredients are sodium bicarbonate, calcium carbonate, aluminum hydroxide, magnesium carbonate, and magnesium hydroxide.
       Sodium bicarbonate, commonly called baking soda, is probably safe and effective for most people. It is the principal antacid in most forms of Alka Seltzer. Overuse of sodium bicarbonate can make the blood too alkaline, a condition called alkalosis. Sodium-

10   containing antacids are not recommended for people who have hypertension (high blood pressure).
       Calcium carbonate is safe in small amounts, but regular use can cause constipation. It also appears that calcium carbonate can actually result in increases acid secretion after a few hours. Tums and many store brand antacids have calcium carbonate as the only active

15   ingredient.
       Aluminum hydroxide, like calcium carbonate, can cause constipation. There is also some concern that antacids containing aluminum ions can deplete the body of essential phosphate ions. Aluminum hydroxide is the active ingredient in Ampojel.
       A suspension of magnesium hydroxide, an antacid, in water is sold as "Milk of

20   Magnesia." Magnesium carbonate is also an antacid. In small doses, magnesium compounds act as antacids, but in large doses, they act as laxatives.
       Many antacid products are composites of antacids. Rolaids and Mylanta contain calcium carbonate and magnesium hydroxide. Maalox has aluminum hydroxide and magnesium hydroxide. These products balance the tendency of magnesium compounds to cause diarrhea

25   with that of aluminum and calcium compounds to cause constipation.
       Although antacids are generally safe for occasional use, they can interact with other medications; and anyone who has severe or repeated attacks of indigestion should consult a physician. Self-medication can sometimes be dangerous.
       (Adapted from Hill, John W. and Kolb, *Doris K. Chemistry for Changing Times, 10th ed.* Upper Saddle River, N.J: Prentice Hall, 2004. 204–205)

28. Which statement best states the main idea for the first paragraph?

   A. Hydrochloric acid produced by the stomach aids in the digestion of food.
   B. There are only a few types of ingredients such as magnesium carbonate, and aluminum hydroxide used in the many brands of antacids.

C. Overeating and anxiety can create a condition of hyperacidity, which can be treated with various antacid products.

D. There are many brands of antacids on the market which can be used to treat hyperacidity.

29. According to this passage, some negative features of the use of antacids include all of the following EXCEPT

A. causing constipation or diarrhea.
B. having interaction of the antacids with other medications, which creates problem with the other medications effectiveness.
C. producing more acid secretion.
D. creating high blood pressure.

30. The author's primary purpose is to

A. inform.
B. criticize.
C. narrate.
D. define.

31. As used in line 22, the word "composites" means

A. substitutions.
B. generics.
C. parts.
D. mixtures.

32. The implied relationship between the sentences of paragraph 5 is

"A suspension of magnesium hydroxide, an antacid, in water is sold as 'Milk of Magnesia.' Magnesium carbonate is also an antacid." (lines 19–20)

A. cause effect.
B. comparison.
C. contrast.
D. definition.

33. "Common ingredients are sodium bicarbonate, calcium carbonate, aluminum hydroxide, magnesium carbonate, and magnesium hydroxide." (lines 5–6)

The relationship of parts within the sentences of above is

A. spatial order.
B. comparison.
C. simple listing.
D. definition.

34. "The stomach secretes hydrochloric acid to aid in the digestion of food." (line 1)

The above sentence is a statement of

A. fact.
B. opinion.

35. In this passage, the author expresses a biased attitude for

A. using the over the counter antacids that balance the problems caused by certain ingredients.
B. using over the counter antacids whenever you have hyperacidity.
C. using caution when using over the counter antacids.
D. overindulging occasionally because products are available to counteract hyperacidity.

36. The author's claim that "Self-medication can sometimes be dangerous." (line 28) is

A. adequately supported by examples.
B. inadequately supported because of lack of evidence.

Answer Key

Pretest

1.	C	10.	C	19.	B	28.	C
2.	B	11.	B	20.	A	29.	D
3.	B	12.	D	21.	A	30.	A
4.	C	13.	A	22.	B	31.	D
5.	C	14.	B	23.	C	32.	B
6.	D	15.	D	24.	B	33.	C
7.	B	16.	A	25.	C	34.	A
8.	B	17.	B	26.	D	35.	C
9.	A	18.	A	27.	D	36.	B

Posttest

Read each passage and answer the questions.

Passage 1

1   Body language is considered by many to be the most "honest" form of communication because of its capacity to express people's real feelings. Body language often reveals a great deal through gestures, eye movement, facial expressions, body positioning and posture, touching behaviors, vocal tone, and use of personal space. Although reading body
5   language is far from an exact science, understanding its basics will help you use it to your advantage as you speak and listen.
       There are some important principals to understand about body language. First, keep in mind that culture influences how body language is interpreted. For example, in the United States, looking away from someone may be a sign of anger or distress; in Japan, the same
10   behavior is usually a sign of respect. In Arab cultures, casual acquaintances stand close together when speaking, while in the United States, the same distance is reserved for intimate conversation. Similarly, in the United States, people get right down to business in meetings, while in Asian cultures, business is preceded by personal conversation that builds trust and relationships. With any cross-cultural conversation, you can discover what seems
15   appropriate by paying attention to what the other person does on a consistent basis. With these things in mind, it is important to understand that nonverbal communication strongly influences first impressions. First impressions emerge from a combination of verbal and nonverbal cues. Nonverbal elements, including tone of voice, eye contact, and speed and style of movement, usually come across first and strongest.
20   Body language can also reinforce or contradict verbal statements. When you greet a friend with a smile and a strong handshake, your body language reinforces your words of welcome. When, on the other hand, your body language contradicts your words, your body generally tells the real story. For example, if right before finals a friend asks how you feel, a response of "fine" is confusing if your arms are folded tightly across your chest and your
25   eyes are averted. These cues communicate tension, not well-being.
       Nonverbal cues can also shade meaning. The statement, *"This is the best idea I've heard all day,"* can mean different things depending on vocal tone. Said sarcastically, the words

158

may mean that the speaker considers the idea a joke. In contrast, the same words said while sitting with your arms and legs crossed and looking away may communicate that you dislike the idea, but are unwilling to say so. Finally, if you maintain eye contact and take the receiver's hand while speaking, you may be communicating that the idea is close to your heart.

The cues mentioned above can help you maximize your awareness of body language so that you can use it—as a speaker and a listener—to your advantage. The key to understanding body language is to pay attention to what other people are really saying through their nonverbal cues and to what you are communicating through your own cues.

(Information and ideas in this passage have been adapted from Carter, Carol, Bishop, Joyce, and Kravits, Sarah Lyman, *Keys to Success in College, Career, and Life,* 4th ed. Upper Saddle River, NJ: Prentice Hall, 2003. 319–321)

1. Which statement best states the main idea for the first paragraph?

   A. Body language is influenced by cultural and religious factors.
   B. Body language can let you know through gestures, facial expressions, body positions, posture, touching behaviors, vocal tone, eye movements, and personal space use what others are feeling.
   C. Because body language can reveal information about a person's feelings and thoughts, understanding it can help you as you speak and listen to others.
   D. Gestures, facial expressions, body positions, postures, touching behaviors, vocal tone, and use of personal space and eye movements are examples of body language.

2. According to the passage, in Japan

   A. looking away from someone is a sign of respect and business is preceded by personal conversation.
   B. looking away from someone is a sign of anger and people stand close together when they converse.
   C. people get right down to business as meetings.
   D. looking away is considered a sign of distress.

3. The author's primary purpose is to

   A. illustrate the uses for body language.
   B. criticize the uses for body language.
   C. inspire us to use body language.
   D. define the term body language.

4. As used in line 25, the word "averted" means looking

   A. unfocused.
   B. directly at you.
   C. straight ahead.
   D. away.

5. "In Arab cultures, casual acquaintances stand close together when speaking, while in the United States, the same distance is reserved for intimate conversation." (lines 10–12)

   The relationship of parts within the sentence above is

   A. cause effect.
   B. comparison.
   C. contrast.
   D. definition.

6. The implied relationship between the sentences of paragraph 4 (lines 26–28) is

   "The statement, *'This is the best idea I've heard all day,'* can mean different things depending on vocal tone. Said sarcastically, the words may mean that the speaker considers the idea a joke."

   A. spatial order.
   B. comparison.
   C. cause and effect.
   D. definition.

7. The tone of this passage can best be described as

   A. motivating.
   B. sensationalistic.
   C. ambivalent.
   D. distressed.

8. "Although reading body language is far from an exact science, understanding its basics will help you use it to advantage as you speak and listen." (lines 4–6)

   The above sentence is a statement of

   A. fact.
   B. opinion.

9. The author's claim that "keep in mind that culture influences how body language is interpreted" (lines 7–8) is

   A. adequately supported by examples.
   B. inadequately supported because of lack of evidence.

Passage 2

1   The quiet wooded area in and around the J. P. Hall Nature Preserve off Highway 16 in Green Cove Springs, Florida today is a place where animal and plant life is protected, but in 1716 it was home to Fort San Francisco de Pupo, built by the Spanish government to help protect the river crossing and block ships from coming upstream.

5   Historians say that Pupo was first mentioned in 1716 as the place where the trail from the Franciscan Indian Missions in Apalachee, now known as Tallahassee, Florida, and St. Augustine, Florida crosses the river. Hikers and campers now explore trails in this preserve once occupied by Indians and soldiers and, while the actual structure of the fort has long since been destroyed, some signs that it once existed along the St. Johns River still remain.

10   In early January of 1740, Gen. James Oglethorpe captured the fort from the Spanish. A trench, dug by Oglethorpe's army to reinforce the fort, is still visible.

In the 1950s, a group of archeologists and students from the University of Florida uncovered thousands of artifacts in this area. Furthermore, an Indian mound discovered in the area-enabled experts to uncover five different layers of earth, attesting to the age of

15   many of the artifacts found buried in the area. Today, 55,000 artifacts taken from these grounds, including Spanish, Indian and turpentine pottery, are housed in Gainesville, Florida. According to commission members, some of the artifacts date to 1000 B.C.

In 1969, an historical marker was erected recognizing the area as an historical site, but according to Clay County Historic Commission members, the marker disappeared about 20

20   years ago. Recently, members of the commission held a ceremony near the J.P. Hall Nature Preserve to dedicate a replacement marker, but the man who was instrumental in getting the process started for the new marker never got the chance to see the project completed.

George Bardin, a local historian, spent years researching the history of Clay County. Bardin, who died in May of 2002, has been described by friends and relatives as passionate

25   in his efforts to preserve the rich past of the county. It was Bardin who filed the original application with the state in April of 2001 for a replacement marker, having made note years earlier that the site of Fort Pupo had proved to be the most historical place in Northeast Florida.

Bardin's daughter, Shelba Kirkland, said her father would have been pleased to see this

30   project come to fruition. "He really lived this," Kirkland said. "All he ever talked about was Clay County. For him, it was the center of the universe."

Kirkland said that after her father's death, she and other family members found two rooms full of maps, pictures, and papers about Clay County.

"Before his death he was very concerned about his maps and his research getting to the right people," Kirkland said. "It is good to know his work is being carried on."

35   (Note: Information for this passage was taken from an article written by Patti Levine-Brown that appeared in the "River City News" and "Clay County Line" sections of the *Florida Times Union* on January 15, 2003.)

10. Which statement best states the main idea for the passage?

    A. The quiet wooded area in and around the J. P. Hall Nature Preserve in Green Cove Springs, Florida is now a protected area for plant and animal life.

    B. The quiet wooded area in and around the J. P. Hall Nature Preserve in Green Cove Springs, Florida used to be a fort, Fort San Francisco de Pupo.

    C. The site of Fort Pupo in Green Cove Springs, Florida is of interest to many because it is historically important and it is now a nature preserve.

    D. Historical sites in Florida need to be recognized and preserved.

11. The author's primary purpose in the passage is to

    A. narrate Bardin's story of his experiences with the quiet wooded area in and around the J. P. Hall Nature Preserve in Green Cove Springs, Florida.

    B. criticize the treatment of the quiet wooded area in and around the J. P. Hall Nature Preserve in Green Cove Springs, Florida.

    C. clarify why the quiet wooded area in and around the J. P. Hall Nature Preserve in Green Cove Springs, Florida is important.

    D. persuade us to value historical places like the quiet wooded area in and around the J. P. Hall Nature Preserve in Green Cove Springs, Florida.

12. The fourth paragraph is organized by

    A. comparison.

    B. contrast.

    C. generalization and example.

    D. time order.

13. The relationship between the sentences of paragraph 3 (lines 12–15) is

"In the 1950s, a group of archeologists and students from the University of Florida uncovered thousands of artifacts in this area. Furthermore, an Indian mound discovered in the area-enabled experts to uncover five different layers of earth, attesting to the age of many of the artifacts found buried in the area."

    A. comparison.

    B. contrast.

    C. addition.

    D. definition.

14. As used in line 31, the word "fruition" means

    A. growth.

    B. completion.

    C. be planned.

    D. a starting point.

15. "Historians say that Pupo was first mentioned in 1716 as the place where the trail from the Franciscan Indian Missions in Apalachee, now known as Tallahassee, Florida, and St. Augustine, Florida crosses the river." (lines 5–7)

The above sentence is a statement of

A. fact.
B. opinion.

16. In this passage, the author expresses a biased attitude for

A. preserving Florida historical sites and nature preserves.
B. recognizing Fort Pupo as a significant historical site.
C. the importance of preserving and recognizing historical sites.
D. General James Oglethorpe.

17. An inference that can be drawn from this passage is

A. Bardin felt that Fort Pupo was the center of his universe and it should be recognized as important to Florida history.
B. Bardin felt that Florida was the most important place for him and that people did not give it the attention it deserved for historical significance.
C. Bardin felt Clay County was important to his life and he worked diligently to have the fort there recognized for its importance.
D. Bardin was angry with the state for not recognizing Fort Pupo in a public manner.

18. The author's claim that the site of Fort Pupo had proven to be the an important historical place in Northeast Florida (lines 26–29) is

A. adequately supported by evidence.
B. inadequately supported because of lack of evidence.

Passage 3

1   As an interesting exercise, carry a trash bag around for a single day and collect everything you throw away. Most people are surprised to find that the average person in the United States discards almost 5 pounds of paper, metal, plastic, and other materials daily (over a lifetime, that's about 50 tons). For the country as a whole, this amounts to
5   about 1 billion pounds of solid waste each and every day.
    As a rich nation containing people who value convenience, the United States has become a *disposable society*. We consume more products than virtually any other nation on Earth, and much of them have throwaway packaging. The most familiar case is fast food, served with cardboard, plastic, and styrofoam containers that we throw away within
10   minutes. However, countless other products—from film to fishhooks—are elaborately packaged to make the product more attractive to the customer and discourage tampering and theft.
    Consider, too, that manufacturers market soft drinks, beer, and fruit juices in aluminum cans, glass, jars, and plastic containers, which not only consume finite resources

but also generate mountains of solid waste. Then there are countless items intentionally designed to be disposable: pens, razors, flashlights, batteries, even cameras. Other goods, from light bulbs to automobiles, are designed to have limited useful life and then become unwanted junk. As Paul H. Connett, author of "The Disposable Society," points out, even the words we use to describe what we throw away "waste," "litter," "trash," "refuse," "garbage," rubbish"—show how little we value what we cannot immediately use.

Living in a rich society, the average person in the United States consumes 50 times more steel, 170 times more newspaper, 250 times more gasoline, and 300 times more plastic each year than the typical person in India. This high level of consumption means that we in the United States not only use a disproportionate share of the planet's natural resources but also generate most of the world's refuse.

We like to say that we "throw things away." But 80 percent of our solid waste is not burned or recycled and never "goes away." Rather, it ends up in landfills, which are, literally, filling up. Materials in landfills also can pollute groundwater. Although in most places laws now regulate what can be discarded in a landfill, the Environmental Protection agency has identified 30,000 dump sites across the United States containing hazardous materials that are polluting water both above and below the ground. In addition, what goes into landfills all too often stays there, sometimes for centuries. Tens of millions of tires, diapers, and other items that we bury in landfills each year do not decompose and will be an unwelcome legacy for future generations.

Environmentalists argue that we should address the problem of solid waste by doing what many of our ancestors did: Turn "waste" into a resource. One way to do this is through *recycling*, reusing resources we would otherwise discard. Recycling is an accepted practice in Japan and many other nations, and it is becoming more common in the United States, where we now reuse about 30 percent of waste materials. The share is increasing as laws mandate reuse of certain materials such as glass bottles and aluminum cans. In addition, because our nation has a market-based economy, recycling is bound to increase as it becomes more profitable.

(Marconis, John J., *Society The Basics. 7th ed.* Upper Saddle River, NJ: Prentice Hall, 2004. 424–425)

19. Which statement best states the main idea for the passage?

   A. The United States produces much of the world's refuse and uses many of the world's natural resources because we are a rich nation and we are materialistic.
   B. Recycling is good for the earth because it reuses many of our natural resources and thus saves some of the resources for others in other countries on this earth.
   C. The Unites States uses more natural resources and creates more trash than other countries, so our nation should take measures to save our resources and make less trash.
   D. The nations of the world should embrace the concept of recycling in order to save natural resources and to create less trash.

20. According to the passage, one item that is not made to be "trash in a landfill" is

    A. cameras.
    B. automobiles.
    C. cardboard packaging.
    D. fast food.

21. The author's primary purpose in the passage is to

    A. persuade.
    B. inform.
    C. entertain.
    D. narrate.

22. The second paragraph is organized by

    A. generalization and example.
    B. comparison and contrast.
    C. classification.
    D. spatial order.

23. "Living in a rich society, the average person in the United States consumes 50 times more steel, 170 times more newspaper, 250 times more gasoline, and 300 times more plastic each year than the typical person in India."

    The relationship of parts within the sentences of above is

    A. addition.
    B. comparison.
    C. contrast.
    D. definition.

24. The tone of this passage can best be described as

    A. critical.
    B. mean-spirited.
    C. ironic.
    D. empathetic.

25 A conclusion that can be drawn from this passage is that the author disapproves of

    A. the wastefulness of people in the United States.
    B. fast food in the United States.
    C. the use of gasoline in the United States.
    D. the fishhooks used in the United States.

26. In this passage, the author expresses a biased attitude against

    A. recycling cans and bottles.
    B. land fills.
    C. extraneous packaging.
    D. film and fishhooks.

27. The author's claim that "This high level of consumption means that we in the United States not only use a disproportionate share of the planet's natural resources but also generate most of the world's refuse." (lines 23–25) is

    A. adequately supported by examples.
    B. inadequately supported because of lack of evidence.

Passage 4

1   The Neolithic Revolution placed us on a level at which we might well have remained indefinitely. The forces of nature would never again challenge men and women as they had Paleolithic peoples. In a few places, however, the balance between humans and nature was upset by a new threat, one posed not by nature but by people themselves. Evidence of that threat can be seen in the earliest Neolithic fortifications, built almost 9,000 years ago in
5 the Near East. What was the source of the human conflict that made these defenses necessary? Was it competition for grazing land among herders or for arable soil among farming communities? The basic cause, we suspect, was that the Neolithic Revolution had been too successful. It had allowed population groups to grow beyond the available food supply. This situation might have been resolved in a number of ways. Constant warfare
10 could have reduced the population. Or the people could have united in larger and more disciplined social units for the sake of group efforts—such as building fortifications—that no loosely organized society could achieve on its own.
      We do not know the outcome of the struggle in the region, but excavations may tell us how far the urbanizing process extended. But about 3,000 years later, similar conflicts, on
15 a larger scale, arose in the Nile Valley and again in the plains of the Tigris and Euphrates rivers. The pressures that forced the people in these regions to abandon Neolithic village life may well have been the same. These conflicts created enough pressure to produce the first civilization. To be civilized, after all, means to live as a citizen, a town dweller. (The word civilization derives from the Latin term for city, civilis.) These new societies were
20 organized into much larger units—cities and city-states—that were far more complex and efficient than had ever existed before. First in Mesopotamia and Egypt, somewhat later in neighboring areas, and in the Indus Valley and along the Yellow river in China, people would henceforth live in a more dynamic world. Their ability to survive was challenged not by the force of nature but by human forces, by tensions and dissent arising either within
25 society or as the result of competition between societies. Efforts to cope with such forces have proven to be a far greater challenge than the earlier struggle with nature. The problems and pressures faced by historic societies thus are very different from those faced by people in the Paleolithic and Neolithic eras.
      These momentous changes also spurred the development of new technologies in what

³⁰ we term the Bronze Age and the Iron Age, which, like the Neolithic, are stages, not distinct eras. People first began to cast bronze, an alloy of copper and tin, in the Middle East around 3500 B.C., at the same time that the earliest cities arose in Egypt and Mesopotamia. The smelting and forging of iron were invented about 2000-1500 B.C. by the Hittites, an Indo-European-speaking people who settled in Cappadocia (today's east central Turkey), a ³⁵ high plateau with abundant copper for mineral resources that helped create the conflicts that beset civilizations everywhere.

Adapted from (Janson, H. W. and Anthony, *A Basic History Of Art*, 6th ed. Upper Saddle River Road, N.J: Prentice Hall. 2002. 254)

28. Which statement best states the main idea for the passage?

   A. Pressures in society that started in Neolithic times caused the people to build fortifications and to engage in conflicts.
   B. Pressures in society that started as a result of the Neolithic Revolution changed the manner in which people lived and spurred the people to create new civilizations and inventions.
   C. In Mesopotamia and Egypt, somewhat later in neighboring area, and in the Indus Valley and along the Yellow river in China, people created civilized towns and cities.
   D. New technologies were created because of the cities that had been created in Mesopotamia and Egypt, somewhat later in neighboring area, and in the Indus Valley and along the Yellow River in China.

29. According to the passage, all of the following are indistinct time periods except the

   A. Neolithic era.
   B. Bronze Age.
   C. Iron Age.
   D. Industrial Age.

30. According to the passage, bronze was created

   A. before iron.
   B. after iron.
   C. at the same time as iron.
   D. by the Hittites.

31. The author's primary purpose in the passage is to

   A. narrate.
   B. inform.
   C. describe.
   D. inspire.

32. As used in line 25, the word "dissent" means

   A. agreement.
   B. discord.
   C. demand.
   D. addition.

33. The relationship between the sentences of paragraph 2 (lines 14–17) is

"We do not know the outcome of the struggle in the region, but excavations may tell us how far the urbanizing process extended. But about 3,000 years later, similar conflicts, on a larger scale, arose in the Nile Valley and again in the plains of the Tigris and Euphrates rivers."

A. comparison.
B. contrast.
C. addition.
D. definition.

34. "These conflicts created enough pressure to produce the first civilization. To be civilized, after all, means to live as a citizen, a town dweller." (lines 18–19)

The relationship of parts within the sentence above is

A. comparison.
B. contrast.
C. classification.
D. definition.

35. What is the overall tone of this passage?

A. educational
B. pessimistic
C. nostalgic
D. inane

36. What does the following sentence from paragraph one suggest about the people in the Neolithic times?

"In a few places, however, the balance between humans and nature was upset by a new threat, one posed not by nature but by people themselves." (lines 3–4)

A. Some people in Neolithic times were in danger of extinction because of the extremes of climate.
B. Some people in Neolithic times were endangered because other people were creating problems for them by fighting with them.
C. Some people in Neolithic times had to change the way they lived for reasons created by the population growth and disease.
D. Some people did not have enough food, so they died.

Answer Key

Pretest

1.	C	10.	C	19.	C	28.	B
2.	A	11.	C	20.	D	29.	B
3.	A	12.	D	21.	A	30.	A
4.	D	13.	C	22.	A	31.	B
5.	C	14.	B	23.	C	32.	B
6.	C	15.	A	24.	A	33.	A

7.	A	16.	B	25.	A	34.	D
8.	B	17.	C	26.	C	35.	A
9.	A	18.	A	27.	B	36.	C

Active and Cooperative Learning

Research done by Terry O'Banion on college learning has brought the concept of active learning to the forefront at educational institutions. Active learning requires student roles to shift from passive to active, thereby; making the students become fully responsible for their own learning. Active learning promotes teachers as learning facilitators who create an environment that is conducive to learning and guides students toward projected outcomes. One of the most widely used techniques that promotes active learning in the classroom is cooperative learning. This teaching and learning strategy has gained prominence at educational institutions throughout the United States. The technique provides teachers a way to construct a helpful and active learning environment in their classrooms that allows students to gain self-confidence and independence. The Center for Cooperative Learning at the University of Minnesota, headed by David and Roger Johnson, has been involved in training hundreds of full time and adjunct faculty in the foundations and advanced courses of this technique. The Center also provides training in structured controversy and leading a cooperative school. Below is a sample of a Cooperative Instructional Activity for Reading and English.

Jigsaw with Five Readings

Task: To understand and interpret five fables relating to everyday life. (This activity can also be done with short poems.) Each group establishes the meaning of a fable, and participants must explain it to members of other groups.

Cooperative Group: Formal (this project may take more than one class period)

Group Size: Students are equally divided into 5 groups.

Room arrangement: Group members' chairs are placed in a circle. Students are face-to face, and eye-to-eye.

Materials: Copies of five fables (e.g. "The Crow and the Pitcher"), sets of numbered cards, flip charts, and markers.

Criteria for success: Everyone must understand and be able to explain his or her group's analysis of the fable to the remainder of the class.

Steps

Each group is given a different fable. Each group establishes the meaning of its fable (one product), and each individual in the group must be able to explain it, thereby demonstrating mastery of the material. The consensus is written on a piece of paper.

Members of all five groups then draw a card with a number (1-5) on it and form new groups according to the numbered card they draw (all ones together, twos, threes and so on). Each person in the new group will explain the fable discussed in their first group while the other members listen carefully so all members understand all five fables.

Each group member must understand all the fables and their meanings and agree with them. Any group member can be picked at random to answer questions about any of the five fables.

Reinforcement of social skills: While the groups are engaged in this activity, some of the social skills teachers should be looking for include active participation, group members encouraging one another, group members asking for help or clarification, and elaboration from all group members.

Processing: After the group has finished the activity, ask them to list three things they did well while working together and one thing they could improve upon.

Extension ideas: Over the next two weeks, a seminar is conducted on each fable. After each seminar, each student writes and turns in a one-minute paper on what they got out of the seminar. After all of the seminars are concluded, each student chooses one of the five fables and writes a short paper about the fable, its meaning. and what he or she learned from the experience.

Helping Students Learn How They Learn

There are several learning styles, personality types, and intelligence questionnaires that will allow students to explore what they like and dislike, how they relate to others, and the various ways of giving and receiving information that work best for them. It is important for students to understand their learning and personality styles so they can capitalize on the strengths they have and compensate for difficulties they encounter when studying new and difficult materials. The inventories are also a good way for students to find things out about themselves that will help them zero in on a career path.

Reading instructors may find it helpful to conduct these inventories or questionnaires with students in the classroom, or because many of these surveys and feedback forms can be found online, instructors may consider taking students to the campus library or learning center computer lab to view some of these inventories and questionnaires on the Web. Once students complete a learning styles or personality inventory, or complete an intelligence questionnaire, ask them to write a paragraph about something they discovered about themselves after completing the inventory and/or questionnaire.

Suggested Learning and Personality Inventories

- **VARK,** developed by Neil Fleming and Charles Bonwell was designed to help determine learning styles. If your students take the VARK, which stands for Visual, Aural, Read/Write, and Kinesthetic, it will provide them with information about their preferred learning style and study strategies they can use to capitalize on their strengths.

- **Myers-Briggs Type Indicator**, developed by Isabel Briggs Myers and Katharine Briggs has been used extensively to determine dimensions of type for more than 30 years. Students taking the Myers-Briggs will learn how the indicator uses the following descriptors to explain personality type: extraversion, introversion, sensing, intuition, thinking, feeling, judgment, and perception.

- **Gardner's Multiple Intelligences**, developed by Harvard psychologists Howard Gardner, established eight categories for how people can know and learn. Gardner believes that everyone possesses these intelligences in varying degrees. Students who are assessed using Gardner's Multiple Intelligences will learn about their most dominant and less dominant intelligence. This inventory will also help them discover some of their strengths and preferences. Gardner's eight categories of intelligences include verbal/linguistic, logical/mathematical, visual/spatial, bodily/kinesthetic, musical/rhythmic, interpersonal, intrapersonal, and naturalistic.

Reading and Interest Inventory

NAME _____

1. What do you hope to get from this course?

_____

_____

2. Do you like to read? _____ If so, what kinds of books do you enjoy most?

_____comedy	_____mystery	_____romance
_____western	_____war story	_____historical
_____gangster	_____educational	_____cartoon
_____science fiction	_____short story	_____poetry
_____adventure	_____horror	_____cookbook
_____biography	_____how to	

3. What method of learning do you find most helpful?

_____ lecture _____individualized learning _____games
_____small group _____cooperative learning

4. Do you learn material better by listening or by using books or other visual aids?_____

5. How often do you read each of the following?

Newspapers	_____
Novels	_____
Magazines	_____
Nonfiction books	_____
Others (explain)	

_____

6. What methods do you use to help you better understand what you are reading?

Reread information	_____
Outline information	_____
Annotate in the margins of your book	_____
Look up unfamiliar words	_____
Persist until you understand the information	_____
Leave it for a while and come back later	_____
Ask for help	_____

7. What other courses are you taking this term?_____

_____

8. How many college semester hours have you earned prior to this term?_____

9. What is your current occupation?_____

10. How many hours do you work each week?_____

11. What is your career goal?_____

12. What is your educational goal? _____

13. What is one of your favorite books?_____

_____

14. List the newspapers and magazines you read regularly._____

_____

15. What kinds of movies do you like best?_____

_____

16. What is your favorite T.V. show?_____

_____

17. What do you like to do when you have free time?_____

_____

18. Do you have any children?_____ ages_____

19. Do you have any pets?_____ What kinds?_____

20. Do you have any hobbies?_____

_____

Text Correlation to the Florida State Exit Exam for Reading

General Information

The Florida State Exit Exam for Reading consists of a minimum of 36 multiple-choice items from a state-developed item bank. Chapters 4, 6, 7, 9, and 10 in Empowered Reading focus on skills that are tested on The Florida State Exit Exam for Reading. Tests in chapters 4, 6, 7, 9, and 10 of the Instructor's Resource Manual that accompanies Empowered Reading include questions that follow the same blueprint of the tests items developed by the state of Florida. A percentage breakdown of items for each of the competencies and skills included on the Florida State Exit Exam for Reading is listed below:

Competency and skills	Location of Skill in Empowered Reading
Author's Message	
determines main ideas	Chapter 6
recognizes supporting details	Chapter 6 and Chapter 7
determines the author's purpose	Chapter 9
Structural Relationships	
identifies organizational patterns	Chapter 7
recognizes relationships within a sentence	Chapter 7
recognizes relationships between sentences	Chapter 7
Language	
determines the meaning of words or phrases in context	Chapter 4
detects bias	Chapter 10
recognizes tone	Chapter 9
Reasoning	
distinguishes between fact and opinion	Chapter 9
draws logical inferences and conclusions	Chapter 9
evaluates reasoning	Chapter 10

Directions

Students taking the Florida State Exit Exam for Reading are directed to read passages and sentences and choose the best response for each item. Several test items in the Instructor's Resource Manual for Empowered Reading have been designed to correlate with the following item format that fits with the Florida State Exit Exam for Reading:

1. All items will be multiple-choice.
2. Each item will test only one skill unless otherwise indicated by item specification.
3. Items will have four options unless otherwise indicated by item specifications.
4. Information needed to respond correctly to an item will be provided in the passage or the item stem.
5. Each item will have only one correct answer.

Passages

Several passages in the Instructor's Resource Manual for Empowered Reading primarily those in chapters 4, 6, 7, 9, and 10 have been designed to correlate with the following format, which fits with the Florida State Exit Exam for Reading:

1. The reading level of the passages will be appropriate for students entering the first freshman-level English courses.
2. The passages will not include highly technical vocabulary or require specialized knowledge.
3. Passage included in this text will be of non-fiction discourse on a variety of topics.

Percentage and number of items on the Florida State Exit Exam

Each chapter in the Instructor Resource Manual provides at least two 10-item tests for use by instructors. Many of the test questions, primarily those in chapters 4, 6, 7, 9, and 10, provide instructors with appropriate review material for the Florida State Exit Exam. By providing teachers with a variety of test items for each skill tested on the Florida State Exit Exam for Reading, this manual contains a sufficient amount of test bank items that match the number of items required for testing on the Florida State Exit Exam. The item breakdown by skill is as follows:

Competency and Skills	pct. of items	number of items
Author's Message	34	12
determines main ideas		4
recognizes supporting details		4
determines the author's purpose		4
Structural Relationships	22	8
identifies organizational patterns		2-3
recognizes relationships within a sentence		2-3
recognizes relationships between sentences		2-3
Language	22	8
determines the meaning of words or phrases in context		2-3
detects bias		2-3
recognizes tone		2-3
Reasoning	22	8
distinguishes between fact and opinion		2-3
draws logical inferences and conclusions		2-3
evaluates reasoning		2-3